MW00463237

He Keeps Me Singing:
The Stories Behind The Hymns

Copyright 2018 by Concept Designs

Published by Concept Designs

Unless otherwise noted, all Scripture is taken from English Standard Version (ESV). (2016) Copyright @ 2001 by Crossway Bibles, a publishing ministry of Good News Publishers.

Also used: New International Version (NIV) Copyright @ 1984 by International Bible Society.

ISBN -13: 978-1986569002

Printed in the United States of America

Acknowledgements

First and foremost I would like to thank God. He gave me the words and inspiration to write this book. It has been quite a long and exciting journey. In the process of putting this book together, I have learned so much. While I was writing to you, His words were speaking to me. I could've never gotten this book done without the grace and wisdom of my Great Redeemer.

I want to thank my family for their encouragement and continual prayers. I also want to thank my Mother and Grandmother for editing this book and for their helping spirit.

I want to thank my friends for always encouraging me and always lifting me in prayer.

I would like to give a special thanks to David Rives and Victoria Rowbottom for their unending help and patience with designing my book cover.

May the words in this book be used as a testimony of God's goodness and faithfulness.

He Keeps Me

The stories behind the hymns

Emma Grace Dieterle

Table of Contents

Introduction

Worship the Lord your God and serve Him only.
(Matthew 4:10)

God has put music in our souls and on our lips to praise and magnify His name alone! God alone is worthy of our devotion, praise, and worship. He is our God, our Creator, and we are commanded to praise and worship Him. Psalm 96:9 says, *"Worship the Lord in the splendor of His holiness; tremble before him, all the earth."* Psalm 29:2 says, *"Give unto the Lord the glory due his name; worship the Lord in the beauty of holiness."*

God has called me on this journey to write this book. It is amazing to understand the stories behind these hymns that motivated the authors to write these songs. The Lord used these hymns to change and bless their lives. I pray that these stories would impact our lives and that we may always have a heart to worship and praise God!

A.W. Tozer said, "Without worship, we are miserable." God doesn't want us to be miserable— He has a perfect plan for our lives. He has done so many things to show us that He loves us. He wants us to have hope for a future with Him— He wants us to have eternal life in heaven with Him.

A life of praise and worship fills our deepest needs and amazingly, it also brings great joy to the Lord. Zephaniah 3:17 declares, *"The Lord your God is with you, He is mighty to save.* He will take great delight in you, He will quiet you with his love, he will rejoice over you with singing."

Many people think that praise and worship is only singing songs at church, but it is so much more! It is also a condition of your heart— a willingness to exalt God and yield to His will. Worship is an expression of love and awe to the God, who gives us more than we deserve. Whether you express your worship by singing, playing music, dancing, or in some other way remember that you are called to worship with your every action, every day of your life.

God is holy, loving, and worthy of all our worship and devotion. Roman 12:1-2 says, *"Therefore, I urge you, brothers and sisters, in view of God's mercy, to offer your bodies as a living sacrifice, holy and pleasing to God—this is your true and proper worship. Do not conform to the pattern of this world, but be transformed by the renewing of your mind. Then you will be able to test and approve what God's will is—his good, pleasing and perfect will."* Always.. in whatever season of life you are in seek to worship Him!

The meaning of worship is not really defined in Scripture. The primary Old Testament term translated "worship" means "to bow down... to prostrate oneself" and the primary New Testament term literally means "to kiss toward."

When we worship, we have to do it with a full heart wanting to praise and lift His name up on high! Psalm 150:1 says, *"Praise the Lord. Praise God in his sanctuary; praise him in his mighty heavens."* True worship is a heartfelt expression of love, adoration, admiration, and celebration. It's something that happens in your heart and soul, when you begin to praise God for who He is and thank Him for what He has done.

The best way to illustrate what happens when we worship is to look at the worship experience of one of God's prophets recorded in Isaiah 6.

"In the year that King Uzziah died, I saw the Lord, high and exalted, seated on a throne; and the train of his robe filled the temple. Above him were seraphim, each with six wings: With two wings they covered their faces, with two they covered their feet, and with two they were flying. And they were calling to one another:

"Holy, holy, holy is the Lord Almighty
the whole earth is full of his glory."
At the sound of their voices the doorposts and thresholds
shook and the temple was filled with smoke."

Worship brings an upward look, a glance at God on His throne in all His glory. It refocuses our view of God. It pulls our affection off our idols and puts them onto the Lord. It causes us to remember how good He is, how big, kind, powerful, and loving He is and how Holy He is.

Isaiah 6:5-7 says, *"Woe to me!" I cried. "I am ruined! For I am a man of unclean lips, and I live among a people of unclean lips, and my eyes have seen the King, the Lord Almighty." Then one of the seraphim flew to me with a live coal in his hand, which he had taken with tongs from the altar. With it he touched my mouth and said, "See, this has touched your lips; your guilt is taken away and your sin atoned for."*

Worship brings an inward look. When you see God for who He really is, as Isaiah did, you start to see yourself for who you really are. We start to see things in our heart and in our life that needs to change and it motivates us to live in obedience to God's Word. It creates in us a desire to serve Him. Notice that after Isaiah saw and confessed his sinfulness, he also experienced the mercy, grace, and forgiveness of the Lord Almighty. That's what happens to us in worship. When you are in His presence and worshipping, you are embraced by God's grace and love.

Worship doesn't end there. Isaiah 6:8 says, *"Then I heard the voice of the Lord saying, "Whom shall I send? And who will go for us? And I said, "Here am I. Send me!"* Genuine worship always leads to an outward look— a personal response or action— a desire to be obedient to whatever God calls you to do.

Genuine worship isn't just singing songs and getting a good feeling in your heart. Genuine worship is seeing the Lord for who He really is— His power, His greatness, His holiness, His sovereignty, His love, and His compassion.

Psalm 145:8 says, *"The LORD is gracious and compassionate, slow to anger and rich in love."*

I pray that through this book we would grow in our worship and praise of Him. I pray that we would also would experience His mercy, love, and grace on our lives and in the end, we would have a deeper and stronger relationship with the Lord. Let us praise the Lord, praise Him in the sanctuary, and praise Him in the mighty Heavens! (Psalm 150:1)

Great is Thy Faithfulness

Psalm 36:5
"Your mercy, O Lord, is the heavens; your faithfulness reaches to the clouds."

Thomas Obediah Chisholm was born in a log cabin in Kentucky, in 1866. At age sixteen, he began teaching school, despite the sparse schooling he had. He came to Christ at age twenty-seven under the ministry of evangelist H. C. Morrison and then became a pastor at thirty-six. Chisholm's heath was unstable.He had a couple of different employments.He went from journalism to insurance and eventually focused on evangelism. Through all the ups and down, he discovered new blessings from God every morning. The third chapter of Lamentations became treasured to him.

Lamentations 3:22-23
"His compassion fail not. They are new every morning; Great is Your faithfulness."

Chisholm said that "Great is Thy Faithfulness" did not have a great story behind its composition, but was simply a poem based on these verses and his own life, but he always remembered that God had given him these lyrics to encourage other people. Dr. Will Houghton of the Moody Bible Institute of Chicago discovered it, and would say in chapel, "Well, I think we shall sing "Great is Thy Faithfulness." It became an unofficial theme song for the Institute; and when Houghton died, it was sung at his funeral.

Still, it remained unknown until popularized around the world by George Beverly Shea and the choirs at the Billy Graham Crusades.

When Chisholm was seventy-five, he wrote this in a letter: "My income has not been large at any time due to impaired health in the earlier years which has followed me on until now. Although I must not fail to record here the unfailing faithfulness of a covenant-keeping

God and that He has given me many wonderful displays of His providing care, for which I am filled with astonishing gratefulness." Thomas died in Ocean Park, New Jersey, in 1960. During his lifetime, he wrote 1,200 poems and hymns. He would always say that he had faith and a faithful Savior.. so true!

The hymn was three verses and a chorus. Verse 1 speaks of God's faithfulness revealed in His Word and is adapted from James 1:17 which says, *"Every good and perfect gift is from above, coming down from the Father of light with whom there is no variation or shadow due to change."*

Verse 2 tells us of God's faithfulness revealed in His creation. The seasons, sun, moon, and stars all continue on their courses: perfect, orderly, and quietly. They are guided by God's faithful hand without any help from us.

Verse 3 reminds us of God's faithfulness revealed in our lives. He pardons all our sin, fills us with His peace, assures us of His presence, gives us strength, hope, and blessing too numerous to count! God doesn't need incredibly gifted or famous people to proclaim these truths from His Word; just faithful ones!

In Christ, the steadfast love of God will never cease. Never. His mercies will never come to an end. Never.

They will be new every morning, and He will be *faithful* to bring them to you. If God is your greatest treasure, if God is your number one priority in your life, *Your Portion,* then you can trust in His faithfulness and His great promises. His faithfulness never ends.

Whatever challenges, trials, or disappointments you might be facing right now, this hymn reminds us that God's promises are true, that He never changes, that His compassions never fail, and that his faithfulness to us in Christ is more that good— it's GREAT!

Great is Thy Faithfulness

"Great is Thy faithfulness," O God my Father,
There is no shadow of turning with Thee;
Thou changest not,Thy compassions, they fail not As
Thou hast been Thou forever wilt be.

"Great is Thy faithfulness!"
"Great is Thy faithfulness!"
Morning by morning new mercies I see;
All I have needed Thy hand hath provided—
"Great is Thy faithfulness,"
Lord, unto me!

Summer and winter, and springtime and harvest, Sun,
moon and stars in their courses above, Join with all
nature in manifold witness
To Thy great faithfulness, mercy and love.

Pardon for sin and a peace that endureth,

Thine own dear presence to cheer and to guide;
Strength for today and bright hope for tomorrow,
Blessings all mine, with ten thousand beside!

What A Friend We Have In Jesus

The Lord turns trials into something beautiful. It declares in Isaiah 61:3, *"To appoint unto them that mourn in Zion, to give unto them beauty for ashes, the oil of joy for mourning, the garment of praise for the spirit of heaviness; that they might be called trees of righteousness, the planting of the Lord, that he might be glorified."*

"What a Friend We Have in Jesus" was birthed into our lives in 1855. The Lord allowed one man to go through many trials and out of that pain we received this beautiful song. Many people have been so blessed to have this song through their many trials and pain.

Joseph Scriven was twenty-five years old and was ready to be married. The day before his wedding his finance wanted to meet at the Bann River. Tragedy struck. As his finance approached the river, her horse was spooked and she was catapulted into the water. She drowned before Joseph could save her. He was heart broken.

Joseph sailed to Canada to start a new life. He fell in love again with Eliza Roche. Eliza became ill and died before their wedding. Once more, there was tremendous pain and turmoil in Joseph's heart.

Then, he received word from Ireland that his dear mother was ill. He wrote a letter of comfort and a poem that he entitled, *What a Friend We Have in Jesus*. Scriven's life reveals the faith spoken about in his poem. Years later, when Joseph was ill, his friend found the poem that he had written to his mother. He was very touched by it. Thirty years later, Charles Converse put it to music, for our souls to be uplifted through our trials and pain. Joseph Scriven's life was very sad, but his experience with the Lord, during his tribulation encouraged and inspired others.

Joseph had so much faith and endurance through all those trials. In the end, he transformed so many people and the most powerful thing he demonstrated to us is how to glorify the Lord in everything, even through our trials and pain. Even though you maybe in a hard trial just remember that you belong to Christ and you are in His love. Knowing Jesus as our friend is the closest fellowship we will ever know.

John 15:15
"No longer do I call you slaves, or the slave does

not know what his master is doing; but I have
called you friends, for all things that I have heard
from My Father I have made known to you."

I am so thankful that the Lord is our friend and He
will always be there for us!

What A Friend We Have in Jesus

What a friend we have in Jesus,
All our sins and griefs to bear!
What a privilege to carry
Everything to God in prayer!
O what peace we often forfeit,
O what needless pain we bear,
All because we do not carry
Everything to God in prayer.

Have we trials and temptations?
Is there trouble anywhere?
We should never be discouraged,
Take it to the Lord in prayer.
Can we find a friend so faithful
Who will all our sorrows share?
Jesus knows our every weakness,
Take it to the Lord in prayer.

Are we weak and heavy laden,

Cumbered with a load of care?
Precious Savior, still our refuge,
Take it to the Lord in prayer.
Do thy friends despise, forsake thee?
Take it to the Lord in prayer!
In his arms he'll take and shield thee,
Thou wilt find a solace there.

Faith Is The Victory

When we go through trials, we need to have faith. When we have strong faith in the Lord, we will have victory! Scripture says in 1 John 5:4, *"This is the victory that overcommeth the world, even our faith."* John Yates was born in 1837. He had a difficult life, but he knew that if he had faith—victory would come!

John Yates received a license to preach in the Methodist church 1858, when he was 21 years old. The Lord had put a fire in his bones to share the Gospel with everyone that was around him. Yates was married in 1864 and had four sons. All of his family died in the same week from Diphtheria. He had a great deal of hurt and pain in his heart, but he gave that to the Lord. He knew that the Lord had a plan and that he was in His hands.

His mother encouraged him to write poetry, when we has 20. He was published for his encouraging, loving poems. Ira Sankey was an Evangelist and a Gospel singer for the Lord. Ira Sankey encouraged John to write songs. In 1891, Yates wrote that amazing, powerful song *Faith is The Victory*. Since 1891, this song has been encouraging believers. The words to this meaningful hymn are based on solid truth that we all need to stand on.

We all need to have faith. When we are rooted in the Lord and abiding in Christ, our faith will bring victory! Matthew 17:20 states, *"He replied, "Because you have so little faith. Truly I tell you, if you have faith as small as a mustard seed, you can say to this mountain, 'Move from here to there,' and it will move. Nothing will be impossible for you."* Thank you Lord for being our glorious Victor that overcomes the world!

Faith is The Victory

Encamped along the hills of light,
Ye Christian soldiers, rise,
And press the battle ere the night
Shall veil the glowing skies.
Against the foe in vales below,
Let all our strength be hurled;
Faith is the victory, we know,
That overcomes the world.

Chorus:
Faith is is the victory!
Faith is is the victory!
Oh, glorious victory,
That overcomes the world.

His banner over us is love,
Our sword the Word of God;
We tread the road the saints above

With shouts of triumph trod.
By faith they, like a whirlwind's breath,
Swept on o'er ev'ry field;
The faith by which they conquered death
Is still our shining shield.

On ev'ry hand the foe we find
Drawn up in dread array;
Let tents of ease be left behind,
And onward to the fray;
Salvation's helmet on each head,
With truth all girt about,
The earth shall tremble 'neath our tread,
And echo with our shout.

To him that overcomes the foe,
White raiment shall be giv'n;
Before the angels he shall know
His name confessed in heav'n.
Then onward from the hills of light,

Our hearts with love aflame,
We'll vanquish all the hosts of night,
In Jesus' conqu'ring name.

Nearer My God To Thee

As we draw near to God through our trials, He will draw near to us...

James 4:8 declares,
"Come near to God and
He will come near to you."

God is with you every step of the way, through your trials. He is our amazing Comforter...

Sarah Adams and Eliza Adams were born in 1803 and 1805. Sarah aspired to be an actress. She acted for three years in London's Richmond Theater. She was married in 1834 to William Bridges Adams. Shortly after, Sarah's health was failing. She could no longer act.

She was very heartbroken, but God was with her the whole way during this trial. She began to write, instead of acting. She wrote poems and magazine articles.

Eliza was a musician and wrote many tunes for Sarah's poems. In 1841, their pastor, William J. Fox, approached Eliza and Sarah to put together a hymnal. They were overjoyed!

Around that time, the Pastor preaching a sermon on *Genesis 28:20-22 which says, "Then Jacob made a vow, saying, "If Godwill be with me and will keep me on this journey that I take, and will give me food to eat and garments to wear, and I return to my father's house in safety, then the LORD will be my God. "This stone, which I have set up as a pillar, will be God's house, and of all that You give me I will surely give a tenth to You."* The pastor asked Sarah to write a hymn for this passage and Sarah did it with a full heart— all for God's glory!

This song is truly Sarah's testimony for the physical suffering she faced. God answered her prayers to be closer to Him in ways Sarah couldn't have dreamed when she wrote the words to this beautiful song. When the Titanic was sinking in April 14, 1912, the band was playing this touching song "Nearer My God To Thee." So many people have been touched by this heartwarming song.

It is the difficult times and trials that strengthens us. We deeply need God's amazing grace! Through our trials, we will always stay nearer to Thee!

Nearer My God To Thee

Nearer, my God, to thee,
Nearer to thee!
E'en though it be a cross
That raiseth me
Still all my song shall be

Though like the wanderer,
The sun gone down
Darkness be over me,
My rest a stone,
Yet in my dreams I'd be

Then with my waking thoughts
Bright with my praise,
Out of my stony griefs
Bethel I'll raise;
So by my woes to be

Chorus

Nearer, my God, to thee,

Nearer, my God, to thee,

Nearer to thee!

There let the way appear,

Steps unto heav'n;

All that thou sendest me,

In mercy giv'n;

Angels beckon me

Or if, on joyful wing

Cleaving the sky,

Sun, moon, and stars forgot,

Upward I fly,

Still all my song shall be

Trust And Obey

Psalm 84:11-12
*"O Lord Almighty, blessed is the man
who trusts in you."*

Trust and obey for there's no
other way to be happy in Jesus!

We will be blessed, when we obey the Lord
in everything we do!

Daniel Towner was a Christian, music director. Daniel Towner was working at a church in Cincinnati in 1885 at the time D.L. Moody was about to speak about Christ in many cities. D.L. Moody was so impressed with Towner's God-given talents that He urged him to come join his team.

Towner immediately accepted. In 1886, they started to minister together. They were at a Testimony meeting in Brockton, Massachusetts, when a young man rose to speak. His heart had been stirred by the impacting message of the Gospel and the beautiful music that had been played. The young man simply said." I'm not sure- but I am going to trust, and I am going to obey."

Those words remained in Towner's head. He jotted them down and wrote the young man's testimony. He sent it to his reverend, John Sammis, whose heart was moved, by this amazing story. Immediately, Sammis began to write the beautiful song *Trust And Obey* and Daniel Towner composed the music.

Music historian, Al Smith, remembers that Towner had became so discouraged during the process that he threw his music into the trash. His wife found his work and Daniel finished the euphonic melody. His heart has happy and full of joy, because he trusted and obeyed God through it all. Towner's wife said, "I feel the melody you have written is just what is needed to carry the message."

She encouraged him to keep going and through it all glorify the King of Kings.

Life may be difficult and we many not understand why things happen, but when we trust God and listen to Him, we will have peace going through our trials.

Many people have shared their feelings and of how they have been blessed by this wonderful hymn. God can use little things to do amazing things that we couldn't even have imagined.

1 Corinthians 2:9 says,
"However, as it is written: "What no eye has seen, what no ear has heard, and what no human mind has conceived the things God has prepared for those who love him."

Trust And Obey

When we walk with the Lord
in the light of his word,
what a glory he sheds on our way!
While we do his good will,
he abides with us still,
and with all who will trust and obey.

Chorus:
Trust and obey, for there's no other way
to be happy in Jesus, but to trust and obey.

Not a burden we bear,
not a sorrow we share,
but our toil he doth richly repay;
not a grief or a loss,
not a frown or a cross,
but is blest if we trust and obey.

But we never can prove
the delights of his love
until all on the altar we lay;
for the favor he shows,
for the joy he bestows,
are for them who will trust and obey.

Then in fellowship sweet
we will sit at his feet,
or we'll walk by his side in the way;
what he says we will do,
where he sends we will go;
never fear, only trust and obey.

Ring The Bells Of Heaven

This joyful song is like
a harp to one's soul!

George Frederick Root was born in 1820 into a musical family full of talents that only the Lord could have orchestrated. He was ambitious to start life with the Lord and to bring glory to God. He moved to Boston to pursue a musical education. He led choirs in three of Boston's churches. He was as busy as a bee for God! He married in 1845 and moved to New York City to teach music.

He met the famous blind, hymn writer, Fanny Crosby. She gave him much encouragement, which deepened his passion for the Lord.

He started writing hymns and became partners with William Cushing. William Cushing was born is Hingham, Massachusetts on December 31,1823. In his early years, all he wanted to do was spend time in the Lord's presence reading God's Word every minute of the day.

William Cushing was an amazing man of God! He had a passion for the Lord like a spreading, wild fire! In the nineteenth century, he gave his entire life savings to pay for the education of a blind girl. At eighteen, the Lord put a desire in his heart to become a pastor. He became a man of the cloth and found the love of his life in 1854. He loved writing hymns to the Lord. He wrote over three-hundred hymns.

George Root was also writing Civil War hits in the 1860's. One of these hits was published. George sent a copy of this song to William Cushing, but he wasn't yet satisfied with it. He wanted something more. It needed to come alive with the Gospel.

Hebrews 4:12
"For the word of God is alive and active. Sharper than any double-edged sword, it penetrates even to dividing soul and spirit, joints and marrow; it judges the thoughts and attitudes of the heart."

He thought of the joy that is happening in heaven and envisioned the Lord rejoicing and singing over us. All he could express was, "Ring The Bells Of Heaven." Luke 15:10 says, *"In the same way, I tell you, there is rejoicing in the presence of God in heaven."* The words to this beautiful hymn started flowing like a delightful river! James 1:5 says," *When you asked the Lord for wisdom He will give it generously."* George asked and he was filled to the brim with amazing wisdom & beautiful words that only the Lord could have given him!

This song was republished with new words two years later in 1868. This hymn shares with us the perspective of Heaven and how much joy there will be on that beautiful day, when we see the Lord!

Oh what a glorious day that will be,
when we see our Abba Father!

The Lord loves us and He is rejoicing over us today and forever! There is glorious singing and praising going on in Heaven!

Let's be joyful... one day we are going to experience
Heaven and celebrate with the
King of Kings!

Ring The Bells Of Heaven

Ring the bells of heaven! There is joy today,
For a soul, returning from the wild!
See the Father meets him out upon the way,
Welcoming His weary, wand'ring child.

Chorus:
Glory! Glory! How the angels sing; Glory!
Glory! How the loud harps ring!
'Tis the ransomed army, like a mighty sea,
Pealing forth the anthem of the free.

Ring the bells of heaven! There is joy today,
For the wand'rer now is reconciled;
Yes, a soul is rescued from his sinful way!
And is born anew a ransomed child.

Ring the bells of heaven! Spread the feast today!
Angels, swell the glad triumphant
strain! Tell the joyful tidings, bear it far away!
For a precious soul is born again.

I Love To Tell The Story

Arabella Katherine Hankey was born in 1834 to a family that cared for her and loved her. Her father was a wealthy business man and had a heart for the Lord that wanted to please him. Arabella was a woman for God and loved to tell the story of the Gospel and how it can change one's life. In her early years of life, she started a girl's Bible study in her neighborhood. She had a deep and growing passion for the Lord.

Jeremiah 20:9
"His word burns in my heart like a fire. It's like a fire in my bones! I am worn out trying to hold it in! I can't do it!"

She was active in the kingdom of God. She wanted to glorify the Lord in whatever she did. 1 Corinthians 10:31 says, *"So, whether you eat or drink, or whatever you do, do all to the glory of God."* In her early 30s, she came down with a dreadful illness. She was confined to a room, but it was not a room of darkness, but of light. She experienced God's presence in that room. It was of light, not dark! Psalm 26:8 says, *"I love your sanctuary, LORD, the place where your glorious presence dwells."* When she was confined to her bed, she praised the Lord and lifted His name up on high. When she was in the middle of a storm, during her life, she worshiped and praised the Lord with this beautiful song, *"I Love To Tell The Story"*.

William Fischer wrote the tune for *"I Love To Tell The Story"*. He was honored to write the music to this song. He was touched by it. William added the famous chorus to this breath- taking song. It was published in 1875.

When Arabella was sick, she could have been depressed and sad, but from that experience came light by glorifying her Father in Heaven with this hymn. She blessed the Lord with her life. Psalm 34:1 declares, *"I will bless the Lord at all times: his praise shall continually be in my mouth."*
The words she wrote from her sickroom are magnifying the Lord and spreading a fire in our bones. Let's lift up our voices and sing:

"I Love To Tell The Story!"

I Love To Tell The Story

I love to tell the story of unseen things above,
Of Jesus and His glory, of Jesus and His love.
I love to tell the story, because I know 'tis true;
It satisfies my longings as nothing else can do.

I love to tell the story, 'twill be my theme in glory,
To tell the old, old story of Jesus and His love.

I love to tell the story; more wonderful it seems Than
all the golden fancies of all our golden dreams. I love
to tell the story, it did so much for me; And that is just
the reason I tell
it now to thee.

I love to tell the story; 'tis pleasant to repeat
What seems, each time I tell it, more wonderfully
sweet. I love to tell the story, for some have never

heard The message of salvation from God's own holy Word.

I love to tell the story, for those who know it best
Seem hungering and thirsting to hear it like the rest.
And when, in scenes of glory, I sing the new, new song, 'Twill be the old, old story that I have loved so long.

All The Way My Savior Leads

God brings tests in our lives that bring a testimony. Fanny Crosby had every purpose to believe that God didn't care about her. She was born in 1820. She was a healthy and sweet girl, but something devastating happened. The doctor incorrectly prescribed a hot poultice. It made her go blind when she was just six weeks old. As she grew older, there were challenges and trials, but she held tight to the Lord. Thoughts crept into her head and she would wonder why she should live, yet Fanny chose to bless God and not blame Him.

Fanny said: "*It seemed intended by the blessed providence of God that I should be blind all my life, and I thank him for the dispensation. If perfect earthly sight were offered me tomorrow I would not accept it. I might not have sung hymns to the praise of God if I had been distracted by the beautiful and interesting things about me.....If I had a choice, I would still choose to remain blind...for when I die, the first face I will ever see will be the face of my blessed Savior.*"

God poured out blessings upon her life. She wrote over 8,000 hymns and songs throughout her life and had over a hundred million songs printed. Psalm 34:1

declares, *"I will bless the Lord at all times: his praise shall continually be in my mouth."* She continually had the name of Jesus on upon her lips. She lifted the Lord's name up on high and exalted Him!

At one point, Fanny lacked money. She needed five dollars. Where was she going to get it? She knew where to go to find help. Psalm 121:2 says, *"My help comes from the LORD, Who maketh heaven and earth."* Her Heavenly Father cared for her and heard her prayers. Psalm 66:19 says, *"God has surely listened and has heard my prayer."* She got down on her knees and asked God to give her the money.

Minutes after, a man came to her door. She didn't know him, but he wanted to meet her. As he left, he placed a five dollar bill into her hand. She pondered about what had just happened and these words came into her heart: *"All the way my Savior leads me."*

She knew that God had heard her prayers and that He is an all powerful and all loving God. It was a miracle! She told the story in these words, "I have no way of accounting for this except to believe that God put in the head of this good man to bring the money."

Robert Lowry wrote the graceful tune to this graceful and beautiful song. It has touched so many minds and hearts. Who would have known that Fanny Crosby would bless so many people? You never know how God is going to use you. Philippians 2:13 says, *"For it is God who works in you to will and to act in order to fulfill his good purpose."*

Fanny Crosby's testimony reveals that God is always faithful to us and He uses everybody for His glory!No matter what the circumstance and no matter the trial, God hears our prayers and He is with us every hour of the day. The Lord was leading Fanny every step of the way— just like me and you! Psalm 17:6 declares, *"My steps have held fast to your paths."* He leads us all the way!

All The Way My Savior Leads

All the way my Savior leads me,
What have I to ask beside?
Can I doubt His tender mercy,
Who through life has been my Guide?
Heav'nly peace, divinest comfort,
Here by faith in Him to dwell!
For I know, whate'er befall me,
Jesus doeth all things well;
For I know, whate'er befall me,
Jesus doeth all things well.

All the way my Savior leads me,
Cheers each winding path I tread,
Gives me grace for every trial,
Feeds me with the living Bread.
Though my weary steps may falter
And my soul athirst may be,
Gushing from the Rock before me,

Lo! A spring of joy I see;
Gushing from the Rock before me,
Lo! A spring of joy I see.

All the way my Savior leads me,
Oh, the fullness of His love!
Perfect rest to me is promised
In my Father's house above.
When my spirit, clothed immortal,
Wings its flight to realms of day
This my song through endless ages:
Jesus led me all the way;
This my song through endless ages:
Jesus led me all the way.

Joy To The World

We have joy, because we have Jesus in our hearts! He gives us everlasting joy.

This beautiful hymn was based on Psalm 98. It was originally titled,"The Messiah's Coming and Kingdom." This song has blessed so many people. We have joy through knowing our Savior.

Psalm 98
"Sing to the Lord a new song,
for he has done marvelous things;
his right hand and his holy arm
have worked salvation for him.

The Lord has made His salvation known
and revealed His righteousness to the nations.

He has remembered his love
and his faithfulness to Israel;
all the ends of the earth have seen
the salvation of our God.

Shout for joy to the Lord, all the earth,
burst into jubilant song with music;

make music to the Lord with the harp,
with the harp and the sound of singing,

with trumpets and the blast of the ram's horn—
shout for joy before the Lord, the King.

Let the sea resound, and everything in it,
the world, and all who live in it.

Let the rivers clap their hands,
let the mountains sing together for joy;

let them sing before the Lord,
for he comes to judge the earth.
He will judge the world in righteousness
and the peoples with equity."

This hymn has become a favorite, during the Christmas season, but it was never intended to be a Christmas carol. The original theme for this song was the second coming of the Lord. *Joy to the World* traces the redemption story throughout history from the promise in the garden to the second coming of our Lord. Our joy is in the finished work of the Lord, whom we praise and glorify!

Isaac Watts wrote this joyful hymn in 1674. He wrote it after he left his pastoral duties, due to a fever. This song was written outside, sitting under a tree in the midst of God's beautiful creation. The exulting words in this song are full of Scriptures. Luke 2:10 says, *"But the angel said to them, "Do not be afraid. I bring you good news that will cause great joy for all the people."* As believers in Christ, this message brings us glorious joy!

As you hear this sweet and beautiful song, think about the words. We should rejoice that we have Jesus in our hearts. Be ready, because He is coming again! What a wonderful day that will be when the whole earth celebrates His appearing. When we are before His throne, we will sing for all eternity, "Repeat the Sounding Joy." Remember that your joy is in your Savior and Lord, who has asked you faithfully to "repeat the sounding joy" of the "wonders of His love" now and forevermore!

Joy To The World

Joy to the world! the Lord is come;
Let earth receive her King;
Let every heart prepare him room,
And heaven and nature sing,
And heaven and nature sing,
And heaven, and heaven, and nature sing.

Joy to the world! the Saviour reigns;
Let men their songs employ;
While fields and floods, rocks, hills, and plains
Repeat the sounding joy,
Repeat the sounding joy,
Repeat, repeat the sounding joy

No more let sins and sorrows grow,
Nor thorns infest the ground;
He comes to make His blessings flow
Far as the curse is found,

Far as the curse is found,
Far as, far as, the curse is found.

He rules the world with truth and grace,
And makes the nations prove
The glories of His righteousness,
And wonders of His love,
And wonders of His love,
And wonders, wonders, of His love.

Safe In The Arms Of Jesus

As Christians we have the assurance that we are safe in His gentle arms. He is our protector. We do not need to fear.

Fanny Crosby was an amazing hymn writer for the Lord. Everyday a new hymn was written for His praise. She quickly wrote about six to seven hymns a day. Throughout her life, Fanny, wrote over eight thousand hymns. God gave her a gift and she quickly put it into practice.

William Doane was the person who put music to the words.   Psalm 108:1 declares, *"My heart, O God, is steadfast; I will sing and make music with all my soul."*

Doane was rushing to catch a train, but before he left, he ran into Fanny's apartment and declared, "Fanny, I want you to write a hymn about "Safe In The Arms Of Jesus." William Doane wanted this song for a Sunday school convention. Time was ticking away and Fanny had only thirty minutes to compose his song, but she declared, "You will have your hymn!" She got her pen and paper out and got right to work. She handed it to Mr. Doane and thanked God for the inspiring words

He gave her. Fanny was smiling with joy. She was so ecstatic and this become her favorite song.

She said, "My heart was in it." Nine years earlier her newborn baby daughter died in her sleep. She was heartbroken, but she knew that everything would be alright, because she was safe in His arms.

Crosby's song spread rapidly into people's hearts. When it was first sung in Charles Spurgeon's Tabernacle in London, the congregation was so touched that they sang it through a second time. It was briskly translated into many foreign languages.

Ira Sankey, an American Gospel singer, shared this song with two little girls. They sang this song while they played with their dolls. One of the girls asked an elder, "How do you know your safe?" The elder responded, "Because I am holding Jesus with both of my hands." The younger girl said, "Ah, but that is not safe. Suppose satan came along and cut your two hands off!" The elder pondered on these thoughts and said, "Oh! I forgot! I forgot! Jesus is holding me with His two hands and satan can't cut His hands off; so I am safe!"

Psalm 94:1 says, "You will be covered by his feathers; under his wings you will be safe: his good faith will be your salvation."

We are in His loving arms and we do not have to worry. When we obey the Lord, we find rest in His arms.

Looking to this broken world for help will not bring us comfort in our trials, but asking God for help brings us closer into loving His arms.

Let's dwell in His safe arms!

Psalm 4:8
"In peace I will lie down and sleep, for you alone, LORD, make me dwell in safety."

Safe In The Arms Of Jesus

Safe in the arms of Jesus,
Safe on His gentle breast,
There by His love o'ershaded,
Sweetly my soul shall rest.
Hark! 'tis the voice of angels
Borne in a song to me,
Over the fields of glory,
Over the jasper sea.

Chorus:
Safe in the arms of Jesus,
Safe on His gentle breast,
There by His love o'ershaded,
Sweetly my soul shall rest.

Safe in the arms of Jesus,
Safe from corroding care,
Safe from the world's temptations,

Sin cannot harm me there.
Free from the blight of sorrow,
Free from my doubts and fears;
Only a few more trials,
Only a few more tears!

Jesus, my heart's dear refuge,
Jesus has died for me;
Firm on the Rock of Ages,
Ever my trust shall be.
Here let me wait with patience,
Wait till the night is o'er;
Wait till I see the morning
Break on the golden shore.

'Tis So Sweet To Trust In Jesus

Oh how sweet it is to trust in our Savior! His shadow of love surrounding us provides an intimacy and trust with our Father.

Louisa Stead had a passion on her heart. God gave Louisa a desire to serve Him overseas. *Psalm 37:4 declares, "Take delight in the Lord and he will give you the desires of your heart."* Her heart and home was in Cincinnati. She was busy about doing things for the Lord. She attended several camp meetings in Urbana, Ohio. Hundred's and thousands of people gave their hearts to Jesus.

It was during the camp sing-alongs that Louisa learned Scripture. In one chorus they sang, "If death should come on his pale horse, I would sing, "I am trusting, Lord in Thee."

Louisa's calling to serve overseas, still kept tugging on her heart. She wanted to serve in China, but she was in poor health. She relinquished it to the Lord. She married Mr. Stead in 1875 and had a daughter. The family went on a vacation in 1880. While they were at the beach having a picnic, they heard a cry. Louisa's husband spotted a little boy drowning. He rushed to help, but the boy pulled him under. They both drowned as Louisa and her daughter watched. Grief filled their hearts. God gave her these trials to grow her relationship with the Lord. They grew their trust in Jesus. And held on tight to Him.

Soon after all these trials, Louisa wrote "'Tis So Sweet To Trust In Jesus." This hymn is a testimony of a song birthed through hardship and trials. She remembered her days in the camp meetings, where she learned God's promises. God's promises sustained her through her tribulations. His Word kept her going. Some days Louisa had nothing to eat. Some good soul would feel led to bake a pie, or leave a basket outside her door, so that she and her daughter could have something to eat. Louisa saw this as the grace of God that provided for her in her time of trial and need; through this her faith and trust in God only grew stronger. At times Louisa was concerned if God would provide for her daughter, but always— God was faithful to her!

God granted Louisa's desire to serve overseas. Her passion was alive and she was excited to share His

Good News to the people of China. She also served as a missionary to South Africa and Zimbabwe.

Through the storms, Louisa's life of faithfulness to the Lord inspired her to work on the mission field after her husband's death.

God used Louisa to share His Word. God was with her and He never left her side. Deuteronomy 31:6 says, *"Be strong and courageous. Do not be afraid or terrified because of them, for the LORD your God goes with you; he will never leave you nor forsake you."*

Tis so sweet to trust in Jesus, Just to take Him at His Word. God always keeps His promises. God stirred in Louisa a desire to serve on the mission field and she obeyed Him. He was faithful through it all.

2 Thessalonians 3:3

"But the Lord is faithful. He will establish you and guard you against the evil one."

He is forever faithful to the end!

'Tis So Sweet To Trust In Jesus

'Tis so sweet to trust in Jesus,
Just to take Him at His word;
Just to rest upon His promise;
Just to know, Thus saith the Lord.

Jesus, Jesus, how I trust Him,
How I've proved Him o'er and o'er,
Jesus, Jesus, Precious Jesus!
O for grace to trust Him more.

O how sweet to trust in Jesus,
Just to trust His cleansing blood;
Just in simple faith to plunge me,
'Neath the healing, cleansing flood.

Yes, 'tis sweet to trust in Jesus,
Just from sin and self to cease;
Just from Jesus simply taking

Life, and rest, and joy, and peace.

I'm so glad I learned to trust Thee,
Precious Jesus, Savior, Friend;
And I know that Thou art with me,
Wilt be with me to the end.

Something Beautiful

Ecclesiates 3:11 declares,
"He has made everything beautiful in its' time.
He has also set eternity in the human heart;
yet no one can fathom what God has done from beginning to
end."

When we have trials in our lives and our hearts feel as if we lost everything, God comes around us with loving arms, promising us that He will make everything beautiful in its time. We have to trust and hold on to His promises.

Bill Gaither is the author of this beautiful hymn. He was born in March 28, 1936. He was born into a warm and loving family who cared about him. He went to Anderson College in 1959 and became an English teacher. In 1962, he married his best friend Gloria. He was trying to teach and focus on a music career, but God wanted him to use his time to completely focus on music and glorify Him.

God put it on my heart to tell you why I chose to write about this song. I was on a road trip with my family to Virginia. As we were traveling back to our home in

Florida, we wanted to stop and see the Billy Graham Library. It was an amazing time! I had been a little downhearted the past couple of days and I asked the Lord to bring encouragement to me. We went into their bookstore and I asked one of the ladies up at the front a question. I just started talking to her and God gave me encouragement that day— right when I needed it. I was telling her that I was writing book about hymns and she asked me, if I knew this one... She started singing *this* beautiful song, "Something Beautiful." The Lord touched my heart. He knows our hearts and He cares for us. Whenever you are feeling upset and down, just know He can turn our lives into something beautiful and something good.

God reminded me, that day, that He is able to take my sad spirit, hard times, my confusion, or impossible situations and make something beautiful out of it. He is amazing! All we have to do is tell Him what is on our heart and He takes what we offer to Him and makes it something good. Nothing is too hard for Him.

When I was about ten or eleven years old, I took ballet lessons. I felt it was time for me to go to the next level. The ballet teachers didn't feel I was qualified for the next level. I didn't know what God's plans for me were at that point in my life. I put my feelings aside and sought Jesus. As I sought the Lord in prayer, He told me to stop dance...it was the hardest thing for me to do at that time... I didn't want to listen, but I had to, because I had to be obedient to the Lord. Later that day, I went to Panera Bread with my "Grammy." She was trying to cheer me up and comfort me, but I was so distressed. Then my Grammy said, "What about being a Bible study teacher." I said ,"No"— that was the last thing I wanted to do. I especially did not want to teach in front of a group. After a while, I started to think about what my Grammy had said and God began to work in my heart. I wrote a letter to the Lord and asked Him what to do next. He answered my prayer —"Do a Bible study." As I began to teach God's Word, I let Him make something beautiful of my life and always gave Him all the glory.

God reminds us in Ecclesiastes that He will make everything beautiful in its time. We have to cling tight to His promises. Sometimes when we have trials and we can't see the beauty at that very moment, we have to trust Him. If we let him, He will make something beautiful of our lives!

Something Beautiful

Something beautiful, something good
All my confusion He understood
All I had to offer Him was brokenness and pain but he
made something beautiful of my life

If there ever were dreams
That were lofty and noble
They were my dreams at the start
And hope for life's best were the hopes
That I harbor down deep in my heart
But my dreams turned to ashes
And my castles all crumbled, my fortune turned to
loss So I wrapped it all in the rags of life And laid it at
the cross.

Since Jesus Came Into My Heart

When Jesus comes into our heart, we become new creatures. Old things have become new. 2 Corinthians 5:17 declares, *"Therefore, if anyone is in Christ, the new creation has come: The old has gone, the new is here!"* Question 1 in the Westminster Catechesim asks us, *"What is the chief end of man?"* The answer: *Man's chief end is to glorify God and to enjoy Him forever.* When He comes into our heart, our perspective changes on how we want to live. Our main focus becomes glorifying Him and enjoying Him forever. The human soul is a template shaped for God, who created it do display His glory! We were made for God. We were made to enjoy and delight in Him forever; to truly *live* by loving Him. We are made to live with Him in glory forever. This is what God always intended, but then sin came into the world. We fall short of His glory.

His faithfulness is great when ours isn't. Our failed, flawed, flagrantly sinful attempts to search for life in the wrong places are covered in Christ's righteousness. Our life becomes tuned to His harp of glory and grace. We are forever changed and transformed by His lavished love for us. Our lives are fulfilled, covered, and full in Christ!

Since Jesus Came Into My Heart was written by Rufus Henry McDaniel. He was born in 1850 in Ohio. By the age of nineteen, he was teaching and preaching the Word of God, wherever he could. McDaniel took time every night to journal to his Heavenly Father. McDaniel wrote, "I feel in my soul that God has something for me to do in brightening the experience of struggling souls. My chief desire is to be a blessing, if possible, to by fellow-men through these hymns and thereby glorify God in the name of his dear son 'whose I am and whom I serve." His main desire in life was to serve our Lord Jesus Christ.

He and his wife Margaret had three children, but their youngest son, Herschel died in early 1913. Through the trial of his son's death, Henry experienced a time of deep depression. McDaniel sat down and wrote the words to this hymn as a reminder of maintaining joy, faith, and hope in times of trial. He felt there was no better way to honor his son than to write music about his faith. He sent it to a couple of song publishers, but never heard anything back. He thought they had rejected his hymn.

God worked in amazing ways that McDaniel could have never even imagined. Ephesians 3:20 declares, *"Now to him who is able to do immeasurably more than all we ask or imagine, according to his power that is at work within us."* His hymn was sung at the Billy Sunday's Crusades in 1915. The song became so popular that people began to sing it in the streets.

God used the lyrics of this song to convert an officer of the Philadelphia Police Department. This man convinced many of his fellow officers to attend the service. More then a hundred confessed with their mouth and believed and in their heart that Jesus is Lord (Romans 10:9).

McDaniel served the Lord in a number of churches in Ohio, before retiring. He died on February 13, 1940 having written over a hundred hymns over his lifetime.

The message of this song is that God can bring a wonderful change in your life, if you are saved. If you aren't saved and reading this book, I pray that you would open the Bible, read the Scriptures, and seek the Lord. If you are saved, it is such a blessing, that

Christians, we have every day to glorify the Lord and enjoy Him forever.

Psalm 34:3

"Glorify the Lord with me; let us exalt his name together."

Since Jesus Came Into My Heart

What a wonderful change in my life has
been wrought since Jesus came into my heart! I have
light in my soul for which long I had sought, since
Jesus came into my heart!
Chorus:
Since Jesus came into my heart,
since Jesus came into my heart,
floods of joy o'er my soul like the sea billows roll,
since Jesus came into my heart.

I'm possessed of a hope that is steadfast and sure,
since Jesus came into my heart!
And no dark clouds of doubt now my pathway
obscure, since Jesus came into my heart!

There's a light in the valley of death now for me, since
Jesus came into my heart!
And the gates of the city beyond I can see,

since Jesus came into my heart!

I shall go there to dwell in that city, I know since
Jesus came into my heart!
And I'm happy, so happy, as onward I go,
since Jesus came into my heart!

Speak, O Lord

1 Samuel 3:8
"Speak, Lord, for your servant is listening."

God speaks to us through His written Word, planting it deep within us to transform and conform us into His likeness. As we listen and obey Him, we will become more like Christ.

There is no historical background about this hymn that I was able to find, so I've provided my own thoughts and commentary.

Each time we sit down to read the Word, we need to be asking the Holy Spirit to speak to us. Each time we gather to worship or hear the Word proclaimed, we need to be asking the Lord to help us hear and learn His truths.

We need to desire a change in our lives so that we can live and fulfill His purposes in and through us. This requires a change in our hearts and minds. Usually when God speaks, He is asking us to take a step of faith.

Hebrews 11:1
"Now faith is the substance of things hoped for, the evidence of things not seen."

Sometimes God asks us to do something out of the box that we wouldn't feel comfortable doing. It stretches us in our faith and relationship with the Lord. It grows us deeper in Him. 2 Peter 3:18 says, *"But grow in the grace and knowledge of our Lord and Savior Jesus Christ. To him be glory both now and forever! Amen."*

"Speak, O Lord, and fulfill in us all your purposes for Your glory." I hope that is our daily prayer. I pray that God would put something in all our lives to grow in His grace and knowledge.

Let's grow deeper in Him. Let's share our heart to Him & always give God all the glory!

Colossians 3:17
"And whatever you do, whether in word or deed, do it all in the name of the Lord Jesus, giving thanks to God the Father through him.

Speak O, Lord

"Speak, O Lord, as we come to You
To receive the food of Your Holy Word.
Take Your truth, plant it deep in us;
Shape and fashion us in Your likeness,
That the light of Christ might be seen today
In our acts of love and our deeds of faith.
Speak, O Lord, and fulfill in us
All Your purposes for Your glory.

Teach us, Lord, full obedience,
Holy reverence, true humility;
Test our thoughts and our attitudes
In the radiance of Your purity.
Cause our faith to rise; cause our eyes to see
Your majestic love and authority.
Words of pow'r that can never fail—
Let their truth prevail over unbelief.

Speak, O Lord, and renew our minds;
Help us grasp the heights of Your plans for us—
Truths unchanged from the dawn of time
That will echo down through eternity.
And by grace we'll stand on Your promises,
And by faith we'll walk as You walk with us.
Speak, O Lord, till Your church is built
And the earth is filled with Your glory."

Amazing Grace

"I am not what I ought to be,
I am not what I want to be,
I am not what I hope to be in another world;
but still I am not what I once use to be,
and by the grace of God I am what I am."
- John Newton

Ephesians 1:7 says, *"In Him we have redemption through His blood, the forgiveness of sin, according to the riches of His grace."* John Newton's life was wrought with trials, but God's grace was shed throughout his life.

John Newton was born in London, July 24, 1725. Newton's memories of his young age were of his godly mother, who despite fragile health, devoted herself to nurturing his soul. At her knee, he memorized Bible passages and hymns. Though she died when he was about seven, he would always remember the prayers she said for him everyday. After her death, John went back and forth to boarding school, spent time on the sea wanting to live a good life, but nonetheless fell deeper and deeper into sin.

In 1743, while going to visit friends, Newton was captured and forced into naval service by the Royal Navy. He became a midshipman aboard HMS *Harwich*. At one point, Newton tried to desert and was punished in front of the crew of 350. Stripped to his waist and tied to the grating, he received a flogging of eight dozen lashes and was reduced to the rank of a common seaman. Following that disgrace and humiliation, Newton initially contemplated murdering the captain and committing suicide by throwing himself overboard. He recovered both physically and mentally from this punishment. Later, while *Harwich* was en route to India, he transferred to *Pegasus*, a slave ship bound for West Africa. The ship carried goods to Africa and traded them for slaves to be shipped to the colonies in the Caribbean and North America.

More voyages, dangers, toils, and snares followed. Then, on the night of March 9, 1748, John, at age 23, was jolted awake by a brutal storm that descended too suddenly for the crew to foresee. The ship was caught in a horrendous storm off the coast of Ireland. In the midst of the whirlwind, he found a book on board by Thomas a Kempis entitled, *Imitation of Christ*. When his ship was nearly foundered in the storm, he gave his life to Christ. The next day, in great peril he cried out to the Lord. He later wrote, "That ninth of March is a day much remembered by me; I have never suffered it to pass unnoticed since the year of 1748 - the Lord came from on high and delivered me out of the deep waters." He also recorded in his journal that when all seemed lost and the ship would surely sink, he exclaimed, "Lord have mercy upon us!" Later in his cabin, he reflected upon what he had said and began to believe that God spoke to him in the storm. God's grace began to change his life.

Yet, habits of twenty-two years, don't disappear overnight. God's grace continued to unfold. Newton turned from gambling, drinking, and profanity after his experience in 1748, but continued in the slave trade and in the mistreatment of slaves. He later wrote in life, "I can't consider myself to have been a believer in the full sense of the word, until a considerable time afterwards." He began to read the Bible at this point and learn more about God's love and character. He professed full belief in Christ and surrendered to God's control several months after the storm, but continued slave trading six more years. Newton's slave career ceased, when he retired from seafaring in 1754, after a serious illness. However, he still continued investing in his friend, Joseph Manesty's slave operations.

In 1750, he married Mary Catlett. They had been best friends, since they were infants. Newton never ceased to be amazed at God's work in his life and he frequently admitted that the Lord had used his passionate love for his wife, Mary, as a motive and means for his spiritual development. God uses people in our lives to bring us closer in our walk with Him. Newton adopted his two orphaned nieces, Elizabeth and Eliza Catlett, children of one of his brothers-in-law. They were a close knit family and loved each other dearly.

Newton was a slow learner, but God is a faithful teacher. Newton met preacher George Whitfield through his first job, after seafaring. He enthusiastically followed Whitfield and also met and admired John Wesley. God had stirred his heart to become a man of the cloth. He applied for ordination as a priest in the Church of England in 1757, but he was not accepted into ministry, until 1764. In 1765, Manesty's shipping company went bankrupt and Newton lost his life's savings. God was humbling John Newton's spirit and he began to have a close and passionate relationship with the Lord. 1 Peter 5:6 says, *"Humble yourselves therefore under the mighty hand of God, that he may exalt you in due time."* The Lord was softening his heart, so that his main focus would be on glorifying Him.

The hymn, "Amazing Grace," was first published in 1779. Originally, the title was "Faith's Review and Expectation." It was based on a study he was doing in 1 Chronicles 17:16-17. For Newton, the sermon was quite personal.

Newton spent time in his attic, where he wrote hymns to amplify the message of his sermons. Here's a forgotten verse that Newton added near the end of "Amazing Grace."

The earth shall soon die slow like snow the sun forbear to shine: But God, Who called me hear below, shall be forever mine.

The last verse of Amazing Grace was actually written by Harriet Beecher Stowe, the author of *Uncle Tom's Cabin:*

When we've been there ten thousand years

Bright shining as the sun,
We've no less days to sing God's praise
Than when we've first begun.

God's grace allowed Newton to make amends for his involvement in the slave trade. Newton was influential in William Wilberforce's conversion to Christianity and the two were fast friends for years. Wilberforce's act to abolish the slave trade was signed into law shortly before Newton's death in 1807. Around that time, Newton was known to have said,"My memory is nearly gone, but I remember two things: That I am a great sinner and that Christ is a great Savior!"

God used John Newton's life. The Lord was a patient and a faithful teacher to John and used his life to bless other people through this hymn. Through Newton's dangers and toils, he became one of the most powerful evangelical preachers in British history and the author of hundreds of hymns. We once were lost, but now we are found. We were blind, but now we see. God's grace has been poured out upon all our lives. 1 Corinthians 15:10 declares, "But by the grace of God, I am what I am." Amazing grace...how sweet the sound!

Amazing Grace

Amazing grace! How sweet the sound That saved a
wretch like me! I once was lost, but now am found;
Was blind, but now I see.

'Twas grace that taught my heart to fear,
And grace my fears relieved;
How precious did that grace appear
The hour I first believed.

Through many dangers, toils and snares,
I have already come; 'Tis grace hath brought me safe
thus far, And grace will lead me home.

The Lord has promised good to me, His Word my
hope secures; He will my Shield and Portion
be, As long as life endures.

Yea, when this flesh and heart shall fail,

And mortal life shall cease, I shall possess,
within the veil, A life of joy and peace.

The earth shall soon dissolve like snow,
The sun forbear to shine; But God, who
called me here below, Will be forever mine.

When we've been there ten thousand years,
Bright shining as the sun, We've no less days to
sing God's praise Than when we'd first begun.

Rock of Ages

Psalm 18:2
The Lord is my rock,
my fortress and my deliverer;
my God is my rock, in whom I take refuge,
my shield and the horn of my salvation,
my stronghold.

On November 4, 1740, Augustus Montague Toplady was born in Farnham, England. He was raised by his mother. His father died in battle when Toplady was just a toddler. His friends and relatives disliked him. He felt rejected and unloved.

Augustus had a deep passion for the Lord and at the age of eleven he wrote, "I am now arrived at the age of eleven years. I praise God I can remember no dreadful crime; to the Lord be the glory." By age twelve, he was preaching and sharing the Word to whoever would listen. At age fourteen, God gave him the ability to speak His Word through music and Augustus started writing hymns.

At sixteen, he was soundly converted to Christ while attending a church service in a barn. The text was

Ephesians 2:13, *"But now in Christ Jesus ye who something were far off are made night by the blood of Christ."* Toplady accepted the Lord into his heart and later wrote, "Under the ministry of that dear messenger, and under that sermon, I was brought nigh by the blood of Christ in August, 1756. Strange that I who had so long sat under the means of grace in England, should be brought nigh to God in an obscure part of Ireland, amidst a handful of God's people met together in a barn and under the ministry of one. Surely it was the Lord's doing, and it is marvelous! The excellency of such power must be of God, and cannot be of man."

He attended Trinity College in Dublin and was ordained, when he was twenty-two and then became a deacon. As a young minister, traveling through the rugged country near England's Cheddar Gorge, the clouds bursted and torrential sheets of rain pummeled the earth. Toplady was able to find shelter standing under a rocky overhang. There, protected from the buffeting wind and rain, under this vast rock, Augustus was inspired to write this hymn. The only paper he had to write on was a playing card, but these words have been forever etched on the card. The words were also written on a rock. —"Rock of Ages."

Toplady did not publish this hymn, until 1775, twelve years later.

Toplady fell ill with tuberculosis around 1776 and lived just two more years. He was thirty-eight, when he died . As he would soon see his Savior's face, He proclaimed these words, "My heart beats every day stronger and stronger for His glory. Sickness is no affliction, pain no cause, death isle no dissolution... My prayers are now all converted to praise Him." Through death, he lived the truth of his own words:

> "Whilst I draw this fleeting breath
> When my eye-strings break in death
> When I soar through tracts unknown
> See Thee on thy judgement throne
> Rock of age, cleft for me,
> Let me hide myself in THEE."

In 1866, when a ship sank in the Bay of Biscay, a man was asked what the passengers were doing, when the ship went down. He said that the last he heard were the people singing, *Rock of Ages.*

The Lord is our rock and the only one we can stand on. Psalm 78:35 says, *"And they remembered* that God was their rock, And the Most High God *their Redeemer."* We need to remember that God is our Rock and that He is guiding our lives and it is in Him we take refuge. May we, in all our travels, watch and go where God is leading. Let us hide ourselves in Thee!

Rock of Ages

Rock of Ages, cleft for me,
let me hide myself in thee;
let the water and the blood,
from thy wounded side which flowed,
be of sin the double cure;
save from wrath and make me pure.

Not the labors of my hands
can fulfill thy law's demands;
could my zeal no respite know,
could my tears forever flow,
all for sin could not atone;
thou must save, and thou alone.

Nothing in my hand I bring,
simply to the cross I cling;
naked, come to thee for dress;
helpless, look to thee for grace;

foul, I to the fountain fly;
wash me, Savior, or I die.

While I draw this fleeting breath,
when mine eyes shall close in death,
when I soar to worlds unknown,
see thee on thy judgment throne,
Rock of Ages, cleft for me,
let me hide myself in thee.

Heaven Came Down &

Glory Filled My Soul

Jesus is the only one that fills my soul with His glory. Psalm 16:9 declares,"*Therefore my heart is glad and my tongue rejoices; my body also will rest secure.*" We are glad and rejoicing, because the Lord is in our souls! *Heaven came down and Glory Filled My Soul* is a hymn that has blessed so many believers! The author, John Peterson, had a major influence on Christian music in the 1950's through the 1970's. He wrote over a 1,000 songs and thirty-five cantatas. He sold thousands of copies of his songs, but his favorite was this song that blessed him and touched others with this praise music.

One day there was a meeting with new believers in Christ. One of the attendees, Jim Rose, sprang to his feet and said that his conversion experience with the Lord was like, "Heaven came down and glory filled my soul." Who would have thought that this one expression would become such an inspiring hymn? Right away this phrase touched John Peterson's heart and he thought it would be a wonderful song. A week later, he completed the song. It became his favorite.

This hymn came into our lives in 1961 and has truly blessed my heart and so many others.

My favorite part of this hymn is the chorus. This man was so happy and full of joy that he felt like he was in heaven when he came to the Lord. It's so important to be focused on heaven, because we never know when the Lord is coming back. We need to be ready for Him at any time. It says in scripture in Matthew 24: 36, *"But concerning that day and hour no one knows, not even the angels of heaven, nor the Son, but the Father only."* We need to just focus on the Lord and the wonderful heaven that God is preparing for us! Thank you Lord that you fill our souls with glory, joy and happiness!

Heaven Came Down and Glory Filled My Soul

O what a wonderful, wonderful day - day I will never forget; After I'd wandered in darkness away, Jesus my Saviour I met. O what a tender, compassionate friend - He met the need of my heart; Shadows dispelling, With joy I am telling, He made all the darkness depart.

Chorus:
Heaven came down and glory filled my soul,
When at the cross the Saviour made me whole;
My sins were washed away
And my night was turned to day
Heaven came down and glory filled my soul!

Born of the Spirit with life from above into God's fam'ly divine, Justified fully thru Calvary's love, O what a standing is mine! And the transaction so quickly was made when as a sinner I came, Took of the offer of grace He did proffer He saved me, O praise His dear name!

Now I've a hope that will surely endure after the passing of time; I have a future in heaven for sure, there in those mansions sublime. And it's because of that wonderful day when at the cross I believed; Riches eternal and blessings supernal from His precious hand I received.

In the Garden

The Lord tell us in Scripture that we should be meditating on His Word day and night. Psalm 1:2 says, *"But they delight in the law of the Lord, meditating on it day and night."* Instead of simply reading a passage of His Word, we must read it, close our eyes, visualize the scene, or perhaps even put ourselves in the picture. The author of this hymn obeyed the Lord by meditating on His Word and allowing it to change his heart.

C. Austin Miles was born on January 7, 1868, in New Jersey to Charles and Sara Miller. Charles graduated from the Philadelphia School of Pharmacy in 1889 and in 1891 he married Bertha Haagan. Together, he and Bertha had three children: Charles Jr, Russell, and Kathryn. Charles, a pharmacist, began writing gospel songs and eventually became an editor of hymnals and songbooks. He became a popular music director of camp meetings, conventions, and churches. His hobby was photography. He found his darkroom perfect for developing, not just his photographs, but for his devotional life. In the privacy of the dark room, Miles loved reading his Bible.

One day in March of 1912, while waiting for some film to develop, he opened the Bible to his favorite chapter in John 20 which tells of the story of the first Easter. Miles later said:

> *"As I read it that day, I seemed to be part of the scene... My hands were resting on the Bible while I stared at the light blue wall. As the light faded, I seemed to be standing at the entrance of a garden, looking down a gently winding path, shaded by olive branches. A woman in white, with head bowed, hand clasping her throat as if to choke back her sobs, walked slowly in the shadows. It was Mary. As she came to the tomb, upon which she placed her hand, she bent over to look in and hurried away. John, in flowing robe, appeared, looking at the tomb; them came Peter, who entered the tomb, followed slowly by John. As they departed, Mary reappeared, leaning her head upon her arm at the tomb, she wept. Turning herself, she saw Jesus standing; so did I. I knew it was Him. She knelt before Him, with arms outstretched and looking into his face, cried, 'Rabboni!' "I awakened in full light gripping my Bible,*

with muscles tense and nerves vibrating.
Under the inspiration of this vision, I wrote
as quickly as the words would be formed. The
same evening I wrote the music."

He said of himself, "It is as a writer of gospel song I am proud to be known for. In that way I maybe of the most use to my Master, whom I serve willingly although not as efficiently as is my desire."

May the desire of our heart be to willingly serve our Master. May we hear the words of our Master say to us, "Well done, good and faithful servant!" (Matthew 25:23)

The Good News is that Christ is our Master and the Captain of our souls. To have a soul conquered by the greatest love that exists—- Jesus..is the greatest gift of all. Life is worth living, because He is with us every hour of the day!

The Lord is with us wherever we go. He walks with us and He talks with us and He is tell us we are His own!

In the Garden

I come to the garden alone
while the dew is still on the roses,
and the voice I hear falling on my ear,
the Son of God discloses.

Chorus:
And he walks with me, and he talks with me, and he
tells me I am his own;
and the joy we share as we tarry there,
none other has ever known.

He speaks, and the sound of his voice
is so sweet the birds hush their singing,
and the melody that he gave to me
within my heart is ringing.

I'd stay in the garden with him
though the night around me be falling,

but he bids me go; thru the voice of woe
his voice to me is calling.

The Solid Rock

For no other foundation can anyone lay than that which is laid Christ.
1 Corinthians 3:11

Edward Mote was born into poverty on January 21, 1797. He did not grow up in a Christian home and did not have parents that instilled God's Word in his heart. His parents were pub owners in London in the early 1800s. His parents would not allow a Bible in their house. They never took Edward to church, and he played in the streets many a Sunday. There was no Bible reading in the school he attended. He wrote, "So ignorant was I that I did not know there was a God."

God knew there was an Edward Mote, and the Lord put people in Edward's path to share, with Him, about the Lord. In his youth, Mote apprenticed with a cabinet maker. When he was sixteen, he was influenced by his boss to attend a service at Tottenham Court Chapel and that morning he heard John Hyatt preach. God works in amazing ways! Hyatt's own father had run a pub, and he had been a cabinet maker like   Mote. In the service, he felt the presence of the

Lord and asked Jesus into his heart. He felt peace in his heart and knew he had Savior that loved him.

Mote wrote, "For two years that sin was in me, till extracted by Calvary's blood, under a sermon... one Glorious Friday morning, from 'The Lord hath laid up him the iniquity of us all." He had joy in his heart that day. He surrendered his life to Jesus!

George Whitfield once said, *"I was delivered from the burden that had so heavily suppressed me. The spirit of mourning was taken from me, and I knew what it was to truly rejoice in God my Savior."*

Mote was rejoicing in the Lord! Mote continued his cabinetry work for years, but he, like Hyatt, entered the ministry (though not until 1852, when he was 55).

In 1834, Mote was on his way to work when the thought crossed his mind that he might like to write a song. Before he arrived at his destination, the chorus of "The Solid Rock" had formed in his mind. He wrote four verses by the end of the day, and two more verses by the following week. Mote's original title for this song was "The Immutable basis of a Sinner's Hope."

Before Mote completed the final two verses, he carried the words in process in his pocket. The following week after services, a man asked him to visit the man's dying wife. Mote agreed. When they reached her bedside, the man said he would like to sing a hymn, read Scripture, and pray for his wife. No hymnbook was available, but Mote remembered the sheets in his pocket. They sang Mote's incomplete song right there. The man asked Mote for a copy for his wife, and as he prepared that copy, Mote wrote the final two verses of the song. Those final two verses so touched the dying woman, that Mote realized that others appreciate them too. So, he had a thousand printed for distribution. These early impulsive copies were submitted without Mote's name, but in 1834, Mote published the song under his own name.

Mote wrote nearly a hundred more hymns. In 1852, Edward, at age 55, gave up his carpentry to pastor the Baptist Church in Horsham, Sussex, where he ministered 21 years. He resigned in 1873, in failing health. As he was to soon see his Savior's face, he said, "I think I am going to Heaven. Yes, I am nearing port. The truths I have preached I am now living upon, and they will do to die upon. Ah! The precious blood, which takes away all our sins. It is this, which makes peace with God." God's truth brings us peace. He is our Rock and He holds all things in His Hands.

Psalm 62:2
"Truly he is my rock and my salvation; he is my fortress, I will never be shaken."

These powerful words from this old hymn are filled with such truth and grace.

> My hope is built on nothing less
> than Jesus' blood and righteousness;
> I dare not trust the sweetest frame,
> but wholly lean on Jesus' name.

> Refrain:
> On Christ, the solid rock, I stand;
> all other ground is sinking sand,
> all other ground is sinking sand.

He paid the price on Calvary's cross, took our sin and shame, bore it all, on our behalf, so that we could live free. The power of the Cross and the resurrection of Christ, broke the curse of death and shame.

"In the Cross is salvation; in the Cross is life; in the Cross is protection against our enemies; in the Cross is infusion of heavenly sweetness; in the Cross is strength of mind; in the Cross is joy of spirit; in the Cross is excellence of virtue; in the Cross is perfection of holiness. There is no salvation of soul, nor hope of eternal life, without the Cross." ~Thomas à Kempis

His truth remains through all eternity. Jesus is the Rock that won't move. He is safe, loving, gracious, forgiving, faithful, powerful, and strong. His Words are *Truth*— bringing us a joyful heart!

The Solid Rock

My hope is built on nothing less
than Jesus' blood and righteousness;
I dare not trust the sweetest frame,
but wholly lean on Jesus' name.

Chorus:
On Christ, the solid rock, I stand;
all other ground is sinking sand,
all other ground is sinking sand.

When darkness veils his lovely face,
I rest on his unchanging grace;
in every high and stormy gale,
my anchor holds within the veil.

His oath, his covenant, his blood
support me in the whelming flood;
when all around my soul gives way,

he then is all my hope and stay.

When he shall come with trumpet sound,
O may I then in him be found,
dressed in his righteousness alone,
faultless to stand before the throne.

Leaning On the Everlasting Arms

The eternal God is your refuge, and underneath are the everlasting arms...
Deuteronomy 33:27

Isn't it a great thought to think that God is supporting us, that God is undergirding us, and that His arms are strong enough to hold us during the difficult times? This truth should provide a refuge for us. In times when relationships disappoint us or finances fail us, it is encouraging to know that there is One who is Everlasting and whose arms are there for us to lean on.

Anthony Showalter was principal of the Southern Normal Musical Institute in Dalton, Georgia. Anthony, a Presbyterian elder, was a well-known advocate of Gospel music. He published over a hundred-thirty music books and sold two million copies. He became known throughout the South for his singing schools in local churches.

Showalter loved to get to know his students and enjoyed keeping up with them as the years passed. One evening in 1887, he was leading a singing school in a local church in Hartselle, Alabama. After dismissing the class for the evening, he gathered his materials and returned home to the his boardinghouse. Two letters had arrived, both from former pupils. Each of the young men were heartbroken, having just lost their wife. Professor Showalter went to the Bible, looking for a verse to comfort them in this time of trial. He selected Deuteronomy 33:27—*"The eternal God is your refuge, and underneath are the everlasting arms."* As he pondered that verse, these words came to his mind:

> *Leaning, leaning, safe and secure from all alarms;*
> *Learning, leaning, safe and secure from all alarms.*

He wrote to his bereaved friends, and then, reaching for another piece of paper, he wrote to his friend, song writer, Elsie Hoffman. He said in his letter, "Here is the chorus for a good hymn from Deuteronomy 33:27. His letter also said, "But I can't come up with any verses." Hoffman wrote three stanzas and sent them back. Showalter set it all to music, and ever since, these words have encouraged us in our adversity.

> *God, the eternal God, is our support at all times, especially when we are sinking into deep trouble.*

These are seasons when we sink quite low...
Dear child of God, even when you are at your lowest,
underneath are the everlasting arms.
—Charles Spurgeon—

The first verses in this song are an exclamation of the great things that God gives to His children, especially as we lean on Him. We get fellowship, joy, blessedness, and peace. Fellowship comes as we become members of His family. In 1 peter 1:8 we are reminded that He gives His followers an "unspeakable joy." Jesus gave us specific instructions on how to live a blessed life in the Sermon on the Mount in Matthew 5. Jesus told us in John 14:27 *"Peace I leave with you; my peace I give you. I do not give to you as the world gives. Do not let you hearts be troubled and do not be afraid."*

In this hymn, there are two different kinds of "What" statements. It says:

What have I to dread, what have I to fear,
Leaning on the everlasting arms.

It says in the Bible 365 times "Do not fear." God knows that our hearts tend to run to fear, during difficult times. Our human reaction is to be afraid.

God knows us and that is why He commanded us so many times "Do not fear." In this hymn, we are reminded that we don't have anything to fear. We don't have anything to dread. We serve a God, who is in control. He is everywhere. He knows everything. He is all powerful. He knows our needs and our concerns and can meet us right where we are.

Have you ever broken your leg, twisted your knee, or sprained you ankle? If so, you probably are familiar with using crutches. When someone says the word "crutch" most of us immediately have negative connotations that come to mind. Crutches are one of those unusual things... They are beneficial, but we don't like them. They help us, but we don't want to use them. Their purpose is good, but if we had our preference, we would prefer not to have them. We like to be independent. Crutches are an outward sign that we have any injury, a problem, or a weakness.

The Apostle Paul tells us in 2 Corinthians 12, about the weakness he had. He referred to it as a "thorn in the flesh." Paul prayed that this weakness would be taken away. He prayed three different times and God chose not to remove the "thorn." He then tells us about an important spiritual truth. The truth that God uses our weaknesses, our flaws, and our personal challenges, and does something extraordinary. He takes His strength and our weakness, and does something awesome. He allows us, in our weakness, to share in His glory and power. Paul then makes the following statement, *"Therefore I will boast all the more gladly about my weakness, so that Christ's power may rest on me."* That is why, for Christ's sake, I delight in weakness, in insults, in hardships, in persecutions and in difficulties. For when I am weak, then I am strong. Delight in weakness? Persecutions? Difficulties? To be honest, we as Christians today struggle with this mindset, but we have to understand that God is giving us truth within these verses of Scripture.

I have a question for all of us- Do we boast about our weaknesses? Do we let others see that we need "crutches" — an outward sign that there are weaknesses in our lives? Do we let others know that we are leaning on God's everlasting arms for support and strength? Are we delighting in the things that might display more of Christ's glory? These are some tough questions. I encourage you today, especially if you are going through a rough time, to look for that opportunity to share Christ, in the midst of your storm. Remember daily that He holds us next to His heart with everlasting arms. We can bring glory to the Lord through our weaknesses.

However low the people of God are at any time brought, everlasting arms are underneath them to keep the spirit from fainting and the faith from failing, even when they are pressed above measure... everlasting arms with which believers have been wonderfully sustained and kept cheerful in the worst of times.
Divine grace is sufficient.
—Matthew Henry—

Let's be bold and share our weaknesses, so that we can bring glory to God. Let's be thankful that we can lean on Him! He is everlasting. He is immutable. In His everlasting arms, we can take refuge!

Leaning on the Everlasting Arms

What a fellowship, what a joy divine,
Leaning on the Everlasting Arms!
What a blessedness, what a peace is mine,
Leaning on the Everlasting Arms!

Leaning, leaning,
Safe and secure from all alarms;
Leaning, leaning,
Leaning on the Everlasting Arms.

O how sweet to walk in this pilgrim way,
Leaning on the Everlasting Arms!
O how bright the path grows from day to day,
Leaning on the Everlasting Arms!
What have I tow dread, what have I to fear,
Leaning on the Everlasting Arms!
I have peace complete with my Lord so near,
Leaning on the Everlasting Arms!

How Firm A Foundation

Fear not, for I am with you; be not dismayed , for I am your
God. I will strength you, Yea, I will help you,
I will uphold you with my righteous right hand.
Isaiah 41:10

John Rippon pastored Carter's Lane Baptist Church in London for sixty-three years, beginning in 1775. He was born in 1751. He was in his mid-twenties, when he first started preaching in the pulpit. He graduate from Baptist College in Bristol, England.

While he was preaching the Lord's Word, John developed a vision for a church hymnal. They would have a hymnal, so that they could sing praises to the Lord and make a joyful noise! He was assisted by his Minister of Music, Robert Keene. It was finally done and was called *A Selection of Hymns from the Best Author, Intended to Be an Appendix to Dr Watts' Psalms and Hymns.* It was published in 1787. Everyone was rejoicing that they had a hymnal so that they could sing to the most holy and beautiful Musician of all! An American edition appeared in 1820.

"How Firm a Foundation" first appeared in the American edition. No one knows its' author, because the line reserved for the author's name simply bore the letter "K." Many scholars attribute the composition to Keene.

The amazing power of this hymn is due to the fact that each of the seven original stanzas were based on various Bible promises. The first verse established the hymnist's theme— God's Word is a sufficient foundation for our faith. The author then selected precious promises from the Bible and converted theses into hymn stanzas:

Fear not, for I am with you; be not dismayed , for I am your
God. I will strength you,
Yes, I will help, I will uphold you with My righteous right
hand.
Isaiah 41:10

When you pass through the waters I will be with you; and
when you pass through the rivers
they will not sweep over you When you walk through the fire
you will not be burned; the flames will not set you ablaze.

Isaiah 43:2
But he said to me, "My grace is sufficient for you, for my power is made perfect in weakness."

Therefore I will boast all the more gladly about my weaknesses, so that Christ's power may rest on me.
2 Corinthians 12:9

Keep your lives free from the love of money and be content with what you have, because God has said, "Never will I leave you; never will I forsake you.
Hebrews 13:5

Regardless of authorship, we know that this hymn was written by a Christian, who understood the promises in God's Word. He most likely stood firm on these promises and held on to them for strength in times of tribulation. In a world obsessed with taking credit for their achievements or receiving payment for their accomplishments, this hymn is an unknown person's offering to the Lord. What intrigues me about this hymn is that after verse one, the entire hymn is God speaking to us.

In the majority of hymns, we sing to God. We sing about God. We sing about each other and we sing about ourselves. In this hymn, God does the talking. He tells us who He is, and how He cares about us, especially during the difficult challenges we are going through. In times of trial, we need to be listening to the Lord. His voice changes the meaning of every hardship. And... in the process, we end up looking more like Jesus.

Verse 1 is God's Word speaking to us:

"How firm a foundation, ye saints of the Lord,
Is laid for your faith in His excellent Word!
What more can He say than to you He hath said,
To you who for refuge to Jesus have fled?"

Verse 2 speaks that God is with us
and we don't have to fear:

"Fear not, I am with thee: O be not dismayed
For I am thy God, and will
still give thee aid; I'll strengthen thee, help thee,
and cause thee to stand, Upheld by my righteous,
omnipotent hand."

In suffering and trials, there is so much temptation to give into the fear and dismay that   may surround us during these trials. God simply becomes an afterthought. Suffering tends to trigger bad reactions — having no hope, weariness, and doubts. However, Isaiah 41:10 offsets those bad reactions with these promises: "I am with you. I am your God. I will strengthen you. I will help you. I will uphold you by my powerful hand." These are the truths we need to be listening to!

The third verse is:
"When through fiery trials your pathway shall lie,
my grace all-sufficient shall be your supply;
the flame shall not hurt you; I only design
your dross to consume and your gold to refine."

It is clear from these verses that not only is God with us in difficult times, but God shows us our purpose. Our significant sufferings ultimately bring about God's purpose, which is a blessing. Romans 8:28 declares, *"And we know that in all things God works for the good of those who love him, who have been called according to his purpose."* God is with us and He can transform us.

Verse four:
"When through the deep waters I call you to go,
the rivers of sorrow shall not overflow,

for I will be with you in trouble to bless,
and sanctify to you your deepest distress.

1 Peter 1:6-9 says, *"In all this you greatly rejoice, though now for a little while you may have had to suffer grief in all kinds of trials. These have come so that the proven genuineness of your faith—of greater worth than gold, which perishes even though refined by fire—may result in praise, glory and honor when Jesus Christ is revealed. Though you have not seen him, you love him; and even though you do not see him now, you believe in him and are filled with an inexpressible and glorious joy, for you are receiving the end result of your faith, the salvation of your souls."*

Peter says emphatically that experiences of suffering purifies our faith and makes it more precious than gold. Suffering is all about transformation. Suffering and trials are used by God to transform our faith. And it is a transformed faith that brings praise, honor, and glory to God.

Verse five:
The soul that on Jesus has leaned for repose
I will not, I will not desert to its foes;
that soul, though all hell should endeavor to shake,
I'll never, no, never, no never forsake!"

God is speaking His truth to us from Deuteronomy 31:6, *"Be strong and courageous. Do not be afraid or terrified because of them, for the Lord your God goes with you; he will never leave you nor forsake you."*

After this hymn was brought to the United States, it was sung to comfort many soldiers on both sides of the Civil War. This sermon in song continues to speak to us throughout our lives.

In the 1800's, God raised up a great general, college administrator, father, and husband. Greatest of all though, he was a humble follower of Christ and devoted Christian.We know him to be...General Robert Edward Lee.

He was a man of faith and prayer and feared the Lord. 2 Samuel 23:3 says, *"He that ruleth over men* must be must, ruling in the fear of God."

Lee was drawn to the great hymns of faith. Worship both sustained and comforted him, during the long days of war. One historian has noted that while others were singing the words during worship, Lee would pray them. His favorite hymn was "How Firm a

Foundation." The congregation at Saint Paul's Church in Richmond, Virginia made it a habit of singing it whenever Lee was present. It was also sung at his funeral in the Washington College Chapel in Lexington, Virginia. He did his best to live a holy life, one pleasing to the Lord. Lee said, "My chief concern is to try to be a humble, earnest Christian…"

The Bible is the Book of Books. - Robert E. Lee

Our Savior says that *"Man does not live by bread alone, but by every word that proceeds out of the mouth of God"*(Matthew 4:4). To a child of God, nothing is more precious than the Holy Word. God's Word was so special for General Lee. Though Lee was a diligent student, most of his adult life was so providentially ordered to leave little time for leisurely reading. He was never too busy; however, to read the Scriptures. He began and ended the day with the Word of God on his mind and heart.

The Scriptures were his comfort and delight:
I prefer the Bible to any other book. There is enough in that to satisfy the most ardent thirst for knowledge; to open the way to true wisdom; and to teach the only road to salvation and eternal happiness. -Robert E. Lee

Lee's pocket Bible was his constant companion in times of peace and war. It had accompanied him since he was a Lieutenant Colonel in the United States Army and was on his bedside, during his final illness in Lexington, Virginia. Its pages were worn out from constant reading. It was what kept him going on.

Lee once remarked that the Scriptures were "Sufficient to satisfy all human desire." One day several English ladies sent him a copy of the Bible. In his letter of thanks, Lee called it "A book in comparison with which all others in my eyes are of minor importance; and which in my perplexities and distresses has never failed to give me light and strength." The Bible was nothing less than his textbook for daily living and the principal means for shaping his beliefs. He constantly sought strength and wisdom from a Source much higher than himself.

God's will ought to be our aim, and I am quite contended that His design should be accomplished and not mine.
— R. E. Lee

Do your duty in all things... You cannot do more; you should never wish to do less. — R. E. Lee

Our duty as Christians is to share the Gospel, love one another, be discipling others and glorifying our Lord. We need to be doing our duty. What does it mean to glorify the Lord? To "glorify" God means to give glory to Him. The word *glory*, related to God in the Old Testament, reveals the idea of greatness of splendor. In the New Testament, the word translated "glory" means "dignity, honor, praise, and worship." Putting the two together, we find that glorifying God means to acknowledge His greatness and give Him honor by praising and worshiping Him, primarily because He— and He alone, deserves to be praised, honored and worshipped. Our main focus should be glorifying the Lord and doing our duty.

What made Lee different from most was that he was saturated with Biblical truth and expressed his faith in God through constant prayer. He was a man, human, frail, and fallible, but he lived in the presence of the Lord. He attempted great things for God and expected great things from God. He totally committed all that he was and all that he had and was looking unto Jesus for everything. He did not merely believe the bank was trustworthy, he made the deposit. He did not just believe in the dependability of the bridge, he crossed over it. He did not merely trust in the sturdiness of the foundation, he built his life upon it.

We need more men and women like General Lee, who want their foundation of life to be built upon God's Word....people who are not only depositories of grace and truth, but also dispensers.

May we live out each day of our lives upon the firm foundation of Jesus Christ our Lord!

1 Corinthians 3:11
"For no one can lay any foundation other than the one already laid, which is Jesus Christ."

How Firm A Foundation

How firm a foundation you saints of the Lord,
    is laid for your faith in his excellent Word!
What more can he say than to you he has said,
    to you who for refuge to Jesus have fled?

"Fear not, I am with you, O be not dismayed,
    for I am your God, and will still give you aid;
I'll strengthen you, help you, and cause you to
stand,upheld by my righteous, omnipotent hand.

"When through the deep waters I call you to go,
    the rivers of sorrow shall not overflow,
    for I will be with you in trouble to bless,
    and sanctify to you your deepest distress.

"When through fiery trials your pathway shall lie,
    my grace all-sufficient shall be your supply;
    the flame shall not hurt you; I only design

your dross to consume and your gold to refine.

"The soul that on Jesus has leaned for repose
I will not, I will not desert to its foes;
that soul, though all hell should endeavor to shake,
I'll never, no, never, no never forsake!"

The Old Rugged Cross

*For God so loved the world that He gave His only begotten
Son, that whoever believes in Him should not perish, but have
everlasting life.*
John 3:16

Jesus Christ is the source— the only source— for our
happiness and it's where we as Christians find joy. We
find peace in our hearts knowing that we will have
eternal life in heaven with our King. We cherish the
old rugged Cross. As Christians, we forget or fail to
remember that Jesus died on the Cross for our sins, so
that we might be forgiven. He laid His life down for
us. John 10:11 says, " *I am the good shepherd; the good
shepherd lays down his life for his friends.*"

George Beverly Shea (The Gospel singer at the Billy
Graham's crusades) remembers seeing George
Bennard, author of this hymn, many times at Winona
Lake Bible Conference in Indiana. He was a heart-
touching preacher and he would sometimes sing, said
Mr. Shea. George Beverly wrote, "His voice was not
trained or out of the ordinary, but he had great feeling
and expression and could really put over any hymn. I
remember how moved I was the first time I heard him

sing his own song "The Old Rugged Cross" and I mediated on these praiseworthy lyrics."

Philippians 4:8
"Brethren whatever things are true, noble, just, pure, lovely of good report and if there is any virtue anything praiseworthy-mediate on the things."

George Bennard was born in Youngstown, Ohio shortly after the end of the Civil War. His father, a coal miner, moved the family to Iowa and there George became a follower of Christ, through the ministry of the Salvation Army. He felt a calling on his heart to train for ministry, but his plans were thwarted, when his father's death left him responsible for his mother and sisters. He was sixteen years old at the time. Instead of seminary, he worked by day, but devoted his spare time to theology.

Eventually, George's obligations lessened and he was able to move to Chicago, marry, and begin in ministry with the Salvation Army. Later, he was ordained by the Methodist Episcopal church and became a traveling evangelist.

On one occasion, after a difficult season of ministry, George realized he needed to better understand the power of the Cross of Christ. He later said, "I was praying for a full understanding of the Cross... I read and studied and prayed... The Christ of the Cross became more than a symbol... It was like seeing John 3:16 leave the printed page, take form, and act out the meaning of redemption. While watching this scene with my mind's eye, the theme of the song came to me."

It took several months for the words to formulate in his mind. As he preached though the Midwest, George would carry the words with him, working on them, polishing them, and sometimes singing them in his meetings. It always blessed the audience to hear the lyrics to this hymn.

At last, he finished his hymn. George went to the home of his friends. Rev. and Mrs. L. O. Boswicks and sang it for them. After the last note, he looked at them and asked, "Will it do?" The Boswicks were so moved that they helped pay the fees to have it printed and it soon began appearing in hymnbooks across America.

Our Savior was first stripped of His clothing and beaten with a whip by the Roman soldiers. This "whip" consisted of twelve, leather cords, which had pieces of bone or metal at the ends. Each whip was capable of cutting or tearing its victim's flesh. (The Roman scourge was particularly brutal and some even died from their beatings.) Part of Jesus' beard was plucked out. Jesus was beaten, He was spat upon, and a crown of thorns was forced down on His head. The Lord was then lead outside the city of Jerusalem to be crucified. There, on Mount Calvary, Jesus was crucified between two thieves. His hands and feet were nailed to the Cross, where He hung in excruciating pain for six hours, until His death.

It was at the Cross that our redemption for sin was paid. His grace and His love for us is abounding. Charles Spurgeon said, "I have a great need for Christ. I have a great Christ for my need." He gives us all that we need. He died on the Cross for our sins. He is our only source for true happiness. Let us look to the Cross. There is power in the name of Jesus!

Chorus:
So I'll cherish the old rugged cross
Till my trophies at last I lay down;

I will cling to the old rugged cross,
And exchange it some day for a crown.

2 Timothy 4:6-8
*For I am already being poured out like a drink offering, and the
time for my departure is near. I have fought the good fight, I
have finished the race, I have kept the faith. Now there is in
store for me the crown of righteousness, which the Lord, the
righteous Judge, will award to me on that day—and not only
to me, but also to all who have longed for his appearing.*

Oh, what a mighty testimony the Apostle Paul leaves
us with. He labored for the Lord and acknowledged
that it was accomplished only by the grace of God that
was within him. 1 Corinthians 15:10 says, *"But by the
grace of God I am what I am, and his grace to me was not
without effect. No, I worked harder than all of them--yet not I,
but the grace of God that was with me."* He cherished the
old, rugged Cross and preached it wherever he went.

As children of God, so should we. In the last days, God
is looking for men and women, like the Apostle Paul,
who are willing to finish their course— well.

Your course may not include having a big ministry, but
every child of God can do their duty, as Christians, and

pray. Prayer is powerful and effective. I have seen the power of prayer in my life. You can pray for America — it's leaders, the church, the lost, and whatever the Lord has placed upon your heart. Secondly, pray for God to use you by His grace. Philippines 2:13 says, *"For God is working in you, giving you the desire and the power to do what pleases him."* Will we fulfill His ministry on earth? Will we obey God's calling on our lives? Will we fight the good fight, finish our course, and keep the faith? Will we "cling to that old rugged Cross," and be faithful to its message, until He calls us home some day and rewards us with a crown of righteousness? I encourage you to follow God's calling on your life and always look to Him! Always look to that old rugged Cross.

The Old Rugged Cross

On a hill far away stood an old rugged cross, The
emblem of suff'ring and shame,
And I love that old cross where the Dearest and Best
For a world of lost sinners was slain.

So I'll cherish the old rugged cross,
Till my trophies at last I lay down;
I will cling to the old rugged cross,
And exchange it some day for a crown.

Oh, that old rugged cross, so despised by the
world, Has a wondrous attraction for me;
For the dear Lamb of God left His glory above,
To bear it to dark Calvary.

In the old rugged cross, stained with blood so
divine, A wondrous beauty I see;

For 'twas on that old cross Jesus suffered and died, To pardon and sanctify me.

I Will Sing of My Redeemer

I will sing the Lord's praise, for he has been good to me.
Psalm 13:6

We, as children of the Lord, should be lifting our voices to Him, because He is good to us!

Philip Paul Bliss was blessed by God as a talented hymn writer. He was born in a log cabin in Clearfield County, Pennsylvania in 1838. At the age of ten, he heard the sounds of a piano for the first time and his imagination began to blossom. At the age of eleven, he left home to work in the lumber camps. At the age of twelve, he came to believe in Jesus Christ our Lord.

Later in life, he became a traveling musician and rode his horse, Old Fanny, from town to town. In 1870, he joined the staff of a Chicago church, as a music director and Sunday school superintendent. In March, 1874, he became the song leader and children's director for the evangelistic campaigns of Major Daniel W. Whittle. During this time, Philip was writing some of America's favorite Gospel songs.

By the end of 1876, Philip needed a break. He had just written the music to "It is Well With My Soul," and finished a plethora of tour meetings with Major Whittle. While he and his wife Lucy were spending the Christmas holiday with his family in Pennsylvania, a telegram arrived requesting they come to Chicago to sing at Moody's Tabernacle on the last Sunday of the year. Although they were tired, Philip and Lucy continued to do the Lord's work.

Bliss and his wife, Lucy, would be traveling extensively, spreading the Gospel in song. While ministering at the meeting, before he left for Chicago, Bliss spoke these words to the congregation: "I may not pass this way again," after which he sang, *I'm Going Home Tomorrow.*" God was speaking to his soul.

On December 29, 1876, leaving their two small children with Philip's mother, they boarded the Pacific Express. The snow was blinding and the eleven-coach train was running about three hours late. About eight o'clock that night, as the train creaked over a chasm near Ashtabula, Ohio, the Trestle bridge collapsed. The engine reached solid ground on the other side of the bridge, but the other car plunged seventy-five feet into the abyss.

Philip survived the crash and crawled out through a window. Within moments, fire broke out, and Lucy was still inside pinned under the twisted metal of the iron seats. The other survivors urged Philip not to crawl back into the flaming wreckage. "If I cannot save her, I will perish with her," he shouted, plunging into the blazing, fiery car. Both Philip and Lucy died. He was thirty- eight.

Philip's trunk finally arrived in Chicago safely. In it were found the words to the last hymns he had written… "I Will Sing of My Redeemer." God used Philip, in a mighty way, to encourage people through his hymns. These songs are a blessing in our walk with the Lord. Don't just sing these words—pray them, speak them and let them bless you!

Let us each day sing of our blessed Redeemer. Singing expresses our heart to Him. Share your heart with Him. A hundred times in Scripture, God says to sing. He wants us to be joyful and glorify our Savior. Psalm 104:33 says, *"I will sing to the LORD all my life; I will sing praise to my God as long as I live."* Let's sing to the Lord and give Him all the honor and praise for He is so worthy.

I Will Sing of My Redeemer

I will sing of my Redeemer
and his wondrous love to me;
on the cruel cross he suffered,
from the curse to set me free.
Sing, O sing of my Redeemer!
With his blood he purchased me;
on the cross he sealed my pardon,
paid the debt, and made me free.

I will tell the wondrous story,
how my lost estate to save,
in his boundless love and mercy,
he the ransom freely gave.
I will praise my dear Redeemer,
his triumphant power I'll tell:
how the victory he gives me
over sin and death and hell.

I will sing of my Redeemer
and his heavenly love for me;
he from death to life has brought me,
Son of God, with him to be.
Sing, O sing of my Redeemer!
With his blood he purchased me;
on the cross he sealed my pardon,
paid the debt, and made me free.

O the Deep, Deep Love of Jesus

For I am convinced that neither death nor life, neither angels nor demons, neither the present nor the future, nor any powers, neither height nor depth, nor anything else in all creation, will be able to separate us from the love of God that is in Christ Jesus our Lord.
Romans 8:38-39

The writer of this hymn painted such a vivid picture of God's love... *Oh, the deep, deep love of Jesus vast, unmeasured, boundless, free! Rolling as a mighty ocean in its fullness over me! Underneath me, all around me, is the current of thy love.* It helps us visualize the immensity of Christ's love, overwhelming and submerging us in the depths of His tender and triumphant heart.

Samuel Trevor Francis was born on November 19, 1834, in a village north of London. His parents soon moved to the city of Hull midway up the English coast. His father was an artist. As a child, Samuel enjoyed poetry and even compiled a little hand-written volume of his own poetry. He also began developing a passion for music and joined the church choir at age nine. As a teenager, he struggled spiritually. When he

144

moved to London to work, he knew things weren't right in his heart.

One day, as he later wrote, "I was on my way home from work and had to cross Hungerford Bridge to the south of the Thames. During the winter's night of wind and rain and in the loneliness of that walk, I cried to God to have mercy on me. I stayed for a moment to look at the dark waters flowing under the bridge and the temptation was whispered to me: 'Make an end of all this misery.' I drew back from the evil thought, and suddenly a message was borne into my very soul: 'You do believe in the Lord Jesus Christ?' I at once answered, 'I do believe,' and I put my whole trust in Him as my Savior."

Francis went on to became a London merchant, but his real passion was Kingdom work especially hymn writing and open air preaching, which occupied his remaining seventy-three years. He traveled widely and preached around the world for the Plymouth Brethren. He died on December 28, 1925, at age ninety-two. God blessed his life and used him to share the Good News!

The rolling melody for this hymn is traditionally called "Ton-Y- Botel" ("Tune in a Bottle") because of a legend that it was found in a bottle along the Welsh Coast. It was actually composed by Thomas J. Williams and first appeared as a hymn tune in 1890 in a Welsh hymnal entitled *Llawlyfn Moliant*.

"Underneath me, all around me" (lyrics in this hymn)—Do you remember learning grammar in school, when you had to learn about prepositional phrases? I get the picture here that the author is trying to communicate, through these phrases, who the Great I Am—truly is. He is around us. He is in us. He is before us. He is behind us. He is under us. He is through us. He is with us. He is near us. Paul wrote in Ephesians that there is *"One God, one Father of all, who is over all, and through all, and in all."* St. Patrick, missionary to Ireland, in the fifth century A.D., wrote of this in a poem proclaiming, "Christ with me, Christ before me, Christ behind me, Christ in me, Christ beneath me, Christ above me, Christ on my right, Christ on my left, Christ where I lie, Christ where I sit, Christ where I arise, Christ in the heart of everyone who thinks of me, Christ in the mouth of every one who speaks to me, Christ in every eye that sees me, Christ in every ear that hears me. Salvation is of the Lord. Salvation is

of the Christ. May your salvation, Lord, be ever with us." This great God who is over all, and in all, and through all, also has His love in our hearts.

"How he loves us, ever loves us, changes never, nevermore!"- The author conveys that God always does love us and that He changes. Lamentations 2:22-23 reminds us, *"Because of the Lord's great love we are not consumed, for his compassions never fail. They are new every morning; great is your faithfulness."* Once again, we see God's unchanging love for His children. He cares for us and He is always faithful! We see a love that is deep, vast, unmeasured, boundless, and free for His precious children!

A relationship with God is like no other relationship you may have experienced. He knows our hearts, He cares and listens to us in all of our concerns. The grace He has poured out upon our lives is not deserved, but He loves us still. His love is unconditional. Jeremiah 31:3 declares, *"I have loved you with an everlasting love; I have drawn you with loving kindness."* He loves you with an everlasting love. You are His child. He knows your heart, your inner thoughts, and He has a deep affection for you!

King David, whom God referred to "as a man after God's own heart" trusted God's love. Psalm 59:16-17 says, *"But I will sing of your strength, in the morning I will sing of your love for you are my fortress, my refuge in times of trouble. You are my strength, I sing praise to you; you, God, are my fortress, my God on whom I can rely."* Let's sing praises to Him and revel in His everlasting love.

The Lord tells us in Scripture that He wants us to believe and rely on His love for us.

Psalm 147: 11 *"The Lord delights in those who fear Him, who put their hope in His unfailing love."*

Psalm 33:18 *"The Lord watches over those who fear Him, those who rely on his unfailing love."*

We need to start relying on His unfailing love and delighting in His presence. God is love. Love is the fundamental essence of His nature and character. God is perfect in love. Let's be deeply rooted in Christ's deep love. Charles Spurgeon once said, "Consider what you owe to His immutability. Though you have changed a thousand times, He has not changed once." His unfailing love for us will never change! How beautiful God's vast love for us is!

"O the Deep, Deep love of Jesus." I believe the author of this hymn did experience deep love that lonely night in London and my prayer for you today is that you experience that deep, deep love as well. As you search the Scriptures and seek Him, look at your heart today and ask Him to show you His love and He will continue to reveal Himself to you. His love is in and through our hearts. God's love for us is unchanging. Psalm 86:15 says, *"But you, O Lord, are a God merciful and gracious, slow to anger and abounding in steadfast love and faithfulness."*

Let us us today rejoice in His abounding, steadfast, deep, deep love!

O the Deep, Deep love of Jesus

Oh, the deep, deep love of Jesus,
vast, unmeasured, boundless, free!
Rolling as a mighty ocean
in its fullness over me!
Underneath me, all around me,
is the current of thy love -
leading onward, leading homeward,
to that glorious rest above!

Oh, the deep, deep love of Jesus -
spread his praise from shore to shore!
How he loves us, ever loves us,
changes never, nevermore!
How he watches o'er his loved ones,
died to call them all his own;
how for them he's interceding,
watching o'er them from the throne!

Oh, the deep, deep love of Jesus,
love of every love the best!
'Tis an ocean vast of blessing,
'tis a haven sweet of rest!

Oh, the deep, deep love of Jesus -
'tis heaven of heavens to me;
and it lifts me up to glory,
for it lifts me up to thee!

Like A River Glorious

… I will extend peace to her like a river…
Isaiah 66:12

In 1876, while vacationing in the south of Wales, Frances Havergal caught a severe cold and suffered inflammation of the lungs. Told she might die, her response was: "If I am really going, it is too good to be true." Her friends were amazed at how peacefully she faced the prospect of dying. That same year, she wrote this hymn.

Like a river glorious is God's perfect peace,
Over all victorious, in its bright increase;
Perfect, yet it floweth fuller every day,
Perfect, yet it groweth deeper all the way.
Stayed upon Jehovah, hearts are fully blest
Finding, as He promised, perfect peace and rest.

Three years later, while meeting some boys to talk with them about the Lord, she ran into cold, wet weather, and became chilled. As her fever grew worse, her family became alarmed. It gradually become apparent that Frances, 42, was dying. On Whitsunday (the seventh Sunday after Easter), as one of her doctors left the room, he said, "Goodbye, I shall not see you again."

"Then you really think I am going?" asked Frances. "Yes." "Today?" "Probably." "Beautiful, " said Frances. "Too good to be true." Soon afterward, she looked up, smiling and said, "Splendid to be so near the gates of heaven!" She asked her brother to sing some hymns to her. He said, "You have talked and written a great deal about the King and you will soon see Him in His beauty." "It's splendid!" she replied. "I thought He would have left me here a long while, but He is so good to take me now."

A little later she whispered, "Come, Lord Jesus, come and fetch me." A terrible rush of convulsions over took her and when they ceased, the nurse gently laid her back on her pillows. Frances' sister later wrote: "Then she looked up steadfastly, as if she saw the Lord. Surely nothing less heavenly could have rejected such a glorious radiance upon her face. For ten minutes we watched that almost visible meeting with her King, her countenance was so glad, as if she were already talking to Him!" Then she tried to sing, but after one sweet, high note she was gone to be with the

Lord. Her voice failed and her brother commended her soul into the Redeemer's hand."

During the days when my grandfather was near death, I realized in these times that I was compelled to run to the Lord and confide in Him more than ever before. I wanted to share with you that dying is beautiful, because there is no more pain, but pure joy— seeing our Saviors face. My family and I read the Psalms to my grandfather. Pouring Scripture over him was the only thing to do. I had been spending time reading Psalm 63:

You, God, are my God,
earnestly I seek you;
I thirst for you,
my whole being longs for you,
in a dry and parched land where there is no water.
I have seen you in the sanctuary
and beheld your power and your glory.

Because your love is better than life,
my lips will glorify you.

This Psalm gave me joy that my grandfather will soon be joined with the Lord. The longing to see Jesus will be gone... as he will be in His presence. My Poppy would soon know that His *love* is so much more amazing than life on this earth. God was calling him to be home.. I would begin to know that the greatest of all miracles is: His love for us!

There is something deeply sacred about knowing that someone you dearly love is about to die. For a little while, time stands still. You cannot leave or do or even think about anything else, so you wait. In those hours, you pray, knowing that it's His will and His timing. All the things we so desperately need to get done are forgotten. The veil between this life and going to Heaven feels thin. Jesus is so close that maybe if we just reach out, we could touch Him and trace the lines on His face with our fingertips. I have never experienced His presence quite as powerfully as I have in the calm and quiet just before He called my grandfather home.

My grandmother and the nurses had a immense responsibility of loving our grandfather as he prepared to meet Jesus. He met us in the stillness of our worshiping and reading the Psalms. There was overwhelming peace surrounding his room. It was Jesus. He was near.

The morning of November the 15th, I could feel it in the air that this was the day. I prayed to the Lord, "Be merciful." I had hoped that it would be an easy passing. The doctor said it would be soon. The Lord had taken the pain he was experiencing away from my grandfather that whole day. God made incredible things happen throughout this day that allowed my grandfather's life to continue to share the truth about the Lord to the very end.

At 5:30 in the evening, my mom felt a sense of urgency and asked us all to sing. My mom chose one of my grandfather's favorite songs...Amazing Grace. After that my grandmother asked me to sing Deuteronomy 6:4. This Old Testament verse is considered the holiest of Jewish prayers. As I finished my last note, Jesus ushered my Poppy into eternity and filled our room with His beautiful peace.

To sit with someone so close to looking upon God's face, just might be the holiest of holy ground. To know that we were with him in that mere moment before he met our Savior, made us feel closer to heaven ourselves. We all knew in our hearts that we were going to miss him, but we knew that he was going to a much more amazing place!

I rejoiced that he was in no more pain. We were there, in the room, as he beheld the face of Jesus for the very first time, and I had the privilege of handing my grandfather straight into His loving arms.

Let's look to His coming, because we never know when the Lord is going to take us. Our time on earth is fleeting. Let us make an impact for the Lord and be bold and courageous for Him! May we live out each day with eternity in our hearts and minds. Let us be longing for our homecoming - when we meet Him face to face!

Like a River Glorious

Like a river glorious is God's perfect peace, over all victorious in its bright increase: perfect, yet still flowing fuller every day; perfect, yet still growing deeper all the way.

Refrain:
Trusting in the Father, hearts are fully blest, finding, as he promised, perfect peace and rest.

Hidden in the hollow of his mighty hand, where no harm can follow, in his strength we stand. We may trust him fully all for us to do; those who trust him wholly find him wholly true.

O For a Closer Walk with God

Colossians 2:6
As you therefore have received Christ Jesus the Lord,
so walk in Him.

William Cowper was just discharged from Cotton's mental Asylum, when he met Morley and Mary Unwin coming out of church. Morley, an evangelical clergyman, invited William to spend two weeks with them and William ended up staying in the Unwin's home for twenty-two years. William took up gardening as a hobby, which helped ward off his depression.

When Morley died after falling off a horse, Mrs. Unwin wanted to sit under the ministry of another evangelical preacher. She decided to move to the village of Olney where there was a population of two-thousand. John Newton was serving the Lord in this village. William moved with her and he and Newton were soon fast friends. William began assisting John in visiting the sick and dying and in distributing benevolent funds.

In December, 1769, Mary Unwin fell ill and appeared to be dying. William's anxiety and depression returned with a vengeance. Mary, being quite a bit older than

William, was a mother-figure to him and he prayed earnestly for her. It was during this time, when examining his own heart, he wrote "O for a Closer Walk with God."

He said, "(Mary) is the chief of blessing I have met with in my journey since the Lord was pleased to call me... Her illness has been a sharp trial to me. Oh, that it may have a sanctified effect.. I began to compose (these verses) yesterday morning before daybreak, but I fell asleep at the end of the first two lines. When I awoke, the third and fourth verses were whispered to my heart in a way I have often experienced."

Fortunately, the danger passed, William's prayers were answered and Mary recovered. God used this trial in William's life to bring him closer to the Lord, to search the Lord, and to seek His heart. The Lord was listening to William's heart and He heard his prayers. Jeremiah 9:12 declares, *"Then you will call on me and come and pray to me, and I will listen to you."* William called upon the Lord and prayed to Him and the Lord listened. He hears our heart and knows your deepest concerns.

God wants us to profit from our trials, to walk with God, weep before God and worship Him. During our trials we need to stay close with the Lord. It is in the midst of our trials that we need to declare, "In everything give thanks." We need to be thankful to God when we are in the shallow and dry lands.

Thanksgiving is recognizing that God is good and understanding the grace He has poured out upon our lives. Be thankful with a full heart. Be a people full of the joy of the Lord.

Philippians 4:4

"Rejoice in the Lord always. I will say it again: Rejoice!"

My prayer for you today is that in your trial, you give thanks for it. Now is the time that you get to trust the Lord, to experience growth in the Lord, and to have a closer walk with God. Charles Spurgeon said, "To trust God in the light is nothing, but to trust Him in the dark— that is faith." Now is our time to trust Him in the dark. Turn your eyes upon Jesus and step into His presence. Let us remember that He is in control of all situations in our lives! God uses trials to mold us into His image. Whether you're facing trials now — or preparing for the trials that will eventually come —

rejoice, knowing that through every hard thing we suffer in life, we share it with Christ.

O For a Closer Walk with God

O for a closer walk with God,
a calm and heavenly frame,
a light to shine upon the road
that leads me to the Lamb!

Where is the blessedness I knew
when first I sought the Lord?
Where is the soul-refreshing view
of Jesus and his Word?

What peaceful hours I once enjoyed!
How sweet their memory still!
But they have left an aching void
the world can never fill.

The dearest idol I have known,
whate'er that idol be,
help me to tear it from thy throne

and worship only thee.

So shall my walk be close with God,
calm and serene my frame;
so purer light shall mark the road
that leads me to the Lamb.

Jesus Loves Me

So that Christ may dwell in your hearts through faith. And I pray that you, being rooted and established in love, may have power, together with all the Lord's holy people, to grasp how wide and long and high
and deep is the love of Christ, and to know this love that surpasses knowledge
—that you may be filled to the measure of all the fullness of God.
Ephesians 3:17-19

Anna and Susan Warner lived in a lovely townhouse in New York City where their father, Henry Whiting Warner was a successful lawyer. The "Panic of 1837" wrecked the family's finances , forcing them to move into a ramshackle Revolutionary War-era home on Constitution (Island on the Hudson) right across from the Military Academy at West Point.

Needing to contribute to the family income, Anna and Susan began writing poems and stories for publication. Anna wrote "Robinson Crusoes's Farmyard," and Susan wrote, "The Wide, Wide World." The girls thus launched literary careers, which resulted in 106 publications and eighteen of them were co-authored.

One of their most successful projects was a novel titled "Say and Seal" in which a little boy named Johnny Fox was dying. His Sunday School teacher, John Linden, comforts, him by taking him in his arms, rocking him and making up a little song: "Jesus loves me, this I know, for the Bible tells me so..."

The novel became a best-seller. When hymn writer William Bradbury read the words of John Lindens's little song (Written by Anna), he composed a childlike tune. "Jesus Love Me," soon became the best-known children's hymn on earth.

Despite their success, the Warner sisters never seemed able to recover from the staggering financial reverses of 1836. Years later a friend wrote, "One day when sitting with Miss Anna in the old living room she took from one of the cases a shell so delicate that it looked like lace work and holding it in her hand, with eyes dimmed with tears, she said, 'There was a time when I was very perplexed, bills were unpaid, necessities must be had, and someone sent me this exquisite thing. As I held it I realized that if God could make this beautiful home for a little creature. He could take care of me.'"

For forty years, Susan and Anna conducted Bible classes for cadets at West Point and both were buried with full military honors. They are the only civilians buried in the military cemetery at West Point. To this day, their home on Constitution Island is maintained by West Point as a museum to their memory.

God took care of them. They would worry, but God had all things in His hands. We may not be in control, but we can trust the One who is. We may not know the future, but we can know the God who does. Isaiah 41:10 says, *""So do not fear, for I am with you; do not be dismayed, for I am your God. I will strengthen you and help you; I will uphold you with my righteous right hand."* The Lord tells us right in His Word to not fear or be dismayed, because we have— Him. He helps us and strengthens us.

Do not fear, because God is our refuge and strength, an ever-present help in trouble (Psalm 46:1).

Jesus loves us...this we know for the Bible tells us so. How can I be so sure of Christ's love? He tells us in

Scripture. His love is not a passing affection, but an abiding, self-sacrificing devotion to His children. He calls us His friends.

John 15:9-17 says, "As the Father has loved me, so have I loved you. Now remain in my love. If you keep my commands, you will remain in my love, just as I have kept my Father's commands and remain in his love. I have told you this so that my joy may be in you and that your joy may be complete. My command is this: Love each other as I have loved you. Greater love has no one than this: to lay down one's life for one's friends. You are my friends if you do what I command. I no longer call you servants, because a servant does not know his master's business. Instead, I have called you friends, for everything that I learned from my Father I have made known to you. You did not choose me, but I chose you and appointed you so that you might go and bear fruit—fruit that will last— and so that whatever you ask in my name the Father will give you. This is my command: Love each other.

The Lord commands us to love each other. Let us remain in His great and merciful love that is bestowed upon us. God calls us to love others, just as He loves us. We show love to others by forgiving, accepting, and honoring them. We can only love others, when we are full of God's love. Today let's show love to one another and be thankful that He first loved us.

Jesus Loves Me

Jesus loves me, this I know,
for the Bible tells me so.
Little ones to him belong;
they are weak, but he is strong.

Chorus:
Yes, Jesus loves me! Yes, Jesus loves me!
Yes, Jesus loves me! The Bible tells me so.

Jesus loves me he who died
heaven's gate to open wide.
He will wash away my sin,
let his little child come in.

Jesus loves me, this I know,
as he loved so long ago,
taking children on his knee,
saying, "Let them come to me."

There Is Power in the Blood

There is none like You, O Lord You are Great,
and Your name is great in might.
Jeremiah:10:6

There is power in the precious name of Jesus. Proverbs 18:10 declares, *"The name of the Lord is a strong tower; the righteous man runs into it and is safe."* The name of the Lord is a strong tower. As Christians, we look to the Lord in everything and He is where we find refuge. All hail the power of Jesus' name!

Both the words and music of this old hymn were written, during a camp meeting at Mountain Lake Park, Maryland, by Lewis Jones. Jones lived in California, graduated from Moody Bible Institute, and spent his vocational life with the Young Men's Christian Association (YMCA). In his free time, he wrote hymns and sang about His precious name. *There Is Power In The Blood,* his best know hymn, is particularly effective in resisting satan's wiles.

One day, as missionary Dick Hillis preached in a Chinese village, his sermon was suddenly interrupted by a sharp, piercing cry. Everyone rushed toward the scream, and Dick's coworker, Mr. Kong, whispered that an evil spirit had seized the man. Dick, having never encountered demon possession, didn't believe him. Just then, a woman rushed toward them. "I beg you help me!" she cried. "An evil spirit has again possessed the father of my children and he's trying to kill himself."

The two evangelists entered the house and stepped over a filthy dog lying in the doorway. The room had a presence of evil encompassing it. "An evil spirit has possessed Farmer Ho," Kong told the witnesses. "Our God, the 'Nothing-He-Cannot-Do One' is more powerful than any spirit and He can deliver this man. First, you must promise you will burn your idols and trust in Jesus, son of the Supreme Emperor."

The people nodded. Kong asked Dick to begin singing the hymn, "There is Power in the Blood." With great hesitation, Dick began to sing, "Would you be free from your burden of sin…" "Now" continued Kong, "in the name of Jesus we will command the evil spirit to leave this man." Kong began praying fervently. 1 John 5:14 says, *This is the confidence we have in approaching God: that if we ask anything according to his will, he hears us.* Suddenly, the old dog in the doorway bolted into the air, screeching, yelping, whirling in circles and snapping wildly at his tail. Kong continued praying and the dog abruptly dropped over dead.

Instantly, Dick remembered Luke 8, where the demons of the Gadarenes invisibly flew into the herd of swine. As Kong finished praying, Farmer Ho seemed quiet and relaxed and was soon strong enough to burn his idols. At his baptism, shortly afterward, he testified, "I was possessed by an evil spirit who boasted he had already killed five people and was going to kill me. But God sent Mr. Kong at just the right moment, and in Jesus I am free."

Christians today fail to remember about the blood of Jesus. The blood is vital and necessary, because the Scripture tell us that without the shedding of the blood, there is no remission of sins. Hebrews 9:22 says, *"In fact, the law requires that nearly everything be cleansed with blood, and without the shedding of blood there is no forgiveness."* It was Jesus who came to this earth and shed His blood at Calvary, making our salvation possible. He willingly was the Perfect Lamb, the sacrifice for our sins and without that sacrifice, we would be eternally lost. It is the power in the blood that free's us from the burden of sin and gives us victory and power for living. There is wonder-working power in the precious blood of the Lamb, Jesus Christ.

Charles Spurgeon— *"I find myself frequently depressed - perhaps more so than any other person here. And I find no better cure for that depression than to trust in the Lord with all my heart, and seek to realize afresh the power of the peace-speaking blood of Jesus, and His infinite love in dying upon the cross to put away all my transgressions."*

When we find ourselves feeling depressed or satan is trying to get a hold of us, we need to stop ourselves and pray in the name of Jesus. To find true peace and happiness, we have to trust in the Lord with all our hearts and seek "the peace-speaking blood of Jesus." Let us be thankful for the infinite love He has for His children. There is power in the blood of the Lamb!

If you are not a believer in Jesus Christ, I pray for you to seek out finding true peace and happiness and that you would ask the Lord to make Himself known to you. I pray that you would search the Scriptures. The Lord is abundantly faithful to us. Leaning into Jesus for help and guidance, I discovered that He alone is my greatest treasure and walking with Him is my greatest joy!

God, who knows each of us before the foundation of the world, calls us uniquely,- not based on anything we have done, but based solely on His irresistible grace. This often begins with Him answering a sincere cry. So, if you don't know Jesus, would you consider praying , "God if you are real, please show me and make yourself apparent to me?" God will show you... through His Word or through speaking to your heart. He is listening...

Scripture says, *"If you declare with your mouth, "Jesus is Lord," and believe in your heart that God raised him from the dead, you will be saved* (Romans 10:9.) I pray that you would discover that walking with the Lord is the greatest joy! We serve a mighty and strong God, who can do *ALL* things! He's so mighty. He can cleanse our wicked hearts and make us white as snow! Praise the Lord!

Praise the Lord we are free from the burden of sin! Thank you Jesus for your grace upon our lives. Lord your name is great in might and it is powerful. There is power, power, wonder-working power in the precious blood of the Lamb. There's wonderful power in the blood. Let us be grateful this day for His wonder-working power in and throughout our lives!

There is Power in the Blood

Would you be free from the burden of sin?
There's power in the blood, power in the blood;
Would you o'er evil a victory win?
There's wonderful power in the blood.

Chorus:
There is power, power, wonder-working power
In the blood of the Lamb.
There is power, power, wonder-working power
In the precious blood of the Lamb.

Would you be free from your passion and pride?
There's power in the blood, power in the blood;
Come for a cleansing to Calvary's tide;
There's wonderful power in the blood.

Would you be whiter, much whiter than snow?
There's power in the blood, power in the blood;

Sin stains are lost in its life giving flow;
There's wonderful power in the blood.

Would you do service for Jesus your King?
There's power in the blood, power in the blood;
Would you live daily His praises to sing?
There's wonderful power in the blood.

Count Your Blessings

Every good and perfect gift is from above, coming down from
the Father of the heavenly lights,
who does not change like shifting shadows.
James 1:17

It's impossible to be thankful and, at the same time, grumpy, cantankerous, critical, or ill-tempered. That's a lesson Johnson Oatman wanted to teach young people through his song, "Count Your Blessings."

Johnson was born in New Jersey just before the Civil War. His father had a powerful voice, which some people claimed was the best singing voice in the East. That's why, as a boy, Johnson Jr. always wanted to stand beside his father in church. When Johnson was a young man, he stood alongside his father in another way. He became a partner in Johnson Oatman & Son, his dad's mercantile business. At age nineteen, Johnson joined the Methodist Episcopal Church and was ordained into the ministry. He often preached, but Johnson never entered the full-time pastorate for he enjoyed the business world and found that it paid his bills, giving him the freedom to minister without a cost.

In 1892, with his father's voice undoubtedly ringing in his memory, Johnson began writing hymns. He averaged two-hundred gospel songs a year— five-thousand, during the course of his lifetime. Among them were: "Higher Ground," "No, Not One," "The Last Mile of the Way," and this one, "Count Your Blessing," which was published in a song book for young people in 1897. It reflected Johnson's faith in the Lord and has been a lesson to many ever since.

A hungry man is more thankful for his morsel than a rich man for his heavily-laden table set before him. A lonely woman in a nursing home will appreciate a visit more than a popular woman with a party thrown in her honor.

If the birds only bursted into song once a year, we'd all pay close attention. But because they are singing every morning, we scarcely bother to listen.

We need to be thankful for every blessing God has given us. Psalm 107:8-9 says, *"Let them give thanks to the Lord for his unfailing love and his wonderful deeds for mankind, for he satisfies the thirsty and fills the hungry with good things.*" Be thankful for every blessing God pours out in your life!

One writer said about Count Your Blessings, "It is like a beam of sunlight that has brightened up the dark places of the earth." Early on, this hymn was especially popular in Great Britain, where it was said, "The men sing it, the boys whistle, the women rock their babies to sleep on this hymn." During the revival in Wales, it was one of the hymns sung at every service.

The wonderful encouragement from "Count Your Blessings" is often misused. It does not mean to deny that you're having problems. It does not mean to ignore your troubling emotions. It does not mean, "Cheer up and act like everything is fine." This hymn is encouraging us to acknowledge openly that we are "tempest-tossed" or "burdened with a load of care" and to bring our concerns to God in prayer. When we count our blessings, it will lead us to joy and peace.

When we go to God with our troubles we can begin to see that we do not need to be discouraged, because "God is over all." In other words, we bring ourselves and our circumstances to the Lord in prayer, because everything is in His hands. To count our blessings means to appreciate, one-by-one, that we have "every spiritual blessing in Christ" (Ephesians 1:3). And genuine thanks and praise to God goes with openly unburdening ourselves before the listening ear of the "Father of compassion" and "God of all comfort."

1 Corinthians 1:3-4 declares, *"Praise be to the God and Father of our Lord Jesus Christ, the Father of compassion and the God of all comfort, who comforts us in all our troubles, so that we can comfort those in any trouble with the comfort we ourselves receive from God."*

Our desire for God is greatly fueled when we need Him most. When we are in trials, that is the time when we need to cling to Him. These trials deepen our prayer life and it's the time when we need to search the Bible for God's promises. Earthly blessings are temporary; they can all be taken away. Job's blessings all disappeared in one fateful day. And yet, in the midst of our painful trials, we can experience God's richest blessings. Our trials ground our faith and bring us into a more intimate relationship with God.

"Blessed rather are those who hear the word of God and keep it!" (Luke 11:28)

*"Blessed is the man who remains steadfast under
trial."* (James 1:12)

*"Blessed are the poor in spirit. . . . Blessed are those who
mourn. . . . Blessed are those who are persecuted for
righteousness' sake . . . Blessed are you when others revile you
and persecute you."* (Matthew 5:3–4, 10–11)

There is no hint of material prosperity or perfect circumstances in any New Testament reference. On the contrary, blessing is typically connected with either poverty and trial. The Greek word translated *blessed* in these passages is *makarioi* which means to be fully satisfied. It refers to those receiving God's favor, *regardless of the circumstances"* What is blessing, then? Scripture shows that blessing is anything God gives that makes us fully satisfied in Him. Anything that draws us closer to Jesus. Anything that helps us relinquish the temporal and hold on more tightly to the eternal. And often it is the struggles and trials, the aching disappointments and the unfulfilled longings that in the end brings us closer to the Lord.

Pain and loss transform us. While they sometimes unravel us, they can also push us to a deeper life with

God than we ever thought possible. They make us rest in God alone.

I invite you to join me by prayerfully reading the lyrics to this great hymn and letting God use it to help you count your blessings today. Ask God to make this sweet song become a beam of light to brighten up any dark places in your life and inspire you to shine the light of Christ more brightly in your circle of influence.

How has God blessed you? What has He done in your life? As the hymn teaches, don't just look to God's physical blessings, but also to His spiritual blessings, which are eternal and are abundantly more meaningful in our lives. 2 Corinthians 9:8 says, *"And God is able to bless you abundantly, so that in all things at all times, having all that you need, you will abound in every good work."* As you "Count Your Blessings," you'll find that "It will surprise you what the Lord has done." I also encourage you to write a prayer of thanks and praise to God. Sharing your heart to Him for all the blessings He has given you. Count your blessings today and always name them one-by-one!

Count Your Blessings

When upon life's billows you are tempest tossed,
When you are discouraged, thinking all is lost,
Count your many blessings, name them one by one,
And it will surprise you what the Lord hath done.

Count your blessings, name them one by one;
Count your blessings, see what God hath done;
Count your blessings, name them one by one;
Count your many blessings, see what God hath done.

Are you ever burdened with a load of care?
Does the cross seem heavy you are called to bear?
Count your many blessings, ev'ry doubt will fly,
And you will be singing as the days go by.

When you look at others with their lands and gold,
Think that Christ has promised you His wealth

untold; Count your many blessings, money cannot buy
Your reward in heaven, nor your home on high.

So, amid the conflict, whether great or small,
Do not be discouraged, God is over all;
Count your many blessings, angels will attend,
Help and comfort give you to your journey's end.

Doxology

Blessed be the God and Father our Lord Jesus Christ,
who has blessed us with every spiritual blessing in the heavenly
places in Christ.
Ephesians 1:3

Thomas Ken has been called "England's first hymnist." He was born in 1637 in Little Berk-hamstead on the fringes of London. When his parents died, he was raised by his half- sister and her husband, who enrolled him in Winchester College. Thomas was later ordained to the ministry and returned to Winchester as a chaplain. Thomas Ken wanted to write a simple, private hymn, not a prominent doxology. "Doxology" comes from the Greek word *doxa,* which means "opinion" or "glory." In the mid-1600s, people started using "doxology" to refer to a short hymn of praise to God. Ken, a bishop in the Church of England, lived in the day, when people thought that only scripture should be the expression of public praise to God, when singing. However, Ken believed that is was very appropriate for people to praise God in their own words, at least in private.

In 1674, Thomas Ken published a book of songs for boys who attended Winchester College, founded in the late 1300s, to educate clergy members. Winchester College is still the oldest public school in England. Ken encouraged the students to use the song for private devotions. Three of these songs were morning, evening, and midnight prayers: "Awake, My Soul and With the Sun," "Glory to Thee, My God, This Night," and "Lord, Now My Sleep Does Me Forsake." All three end with the same line: "Praise God from whom all blessings flow."

Ken exhorted his students, "Be sure to sing the Morning and Evening Hymn in your chamber devoutly, remembering that the Psalmist, upon happy experience, assures you, that it is a good thing to tell of the loving kindness of the Lord early in the morning, and of His truth in the night season." Ken played the lute and sung the hymn in his personal worship each morning.

We need to remember that this beloved, worship stanza was originally attached to simple prayer. Praise should ascend to God not just in worship service, but throughout our day.

Psalm 86:12
"I will praise you, Lord my God, with all my heart; I will glorify your name forever."

Ken lived out practical worship through obedience to God. He was a chaplain to officials and royalty and didn't hesitate to speak up about their wrongdoing. His boldness got him sent away from the royal Dutch court, but it endeared him to King Charles II, who called Ken "the good little man" and said at chapel time, " I must go in and hear Ken tell me my faults." He was not so well received by the two rulers after Charles II and was eventually removed from his position as bishop. He lived out his days in glorifying the Lord and in happy contentment in the home of a friend, refusing to be reinstated by Queen Anne. Before he died, he requested that he be buried at sunrise. His "Morning Hymn" was sung as his body was lowered in the grave.

1 Corinthians 14:26
"What then shall we say, brothers and sisters? When you come together, each of you has a hymn, or a word of instruction, a revelation, a tongue or an interpretation. Everything must be done so that the church may be built up."

The church regularly shared hymns as part of their worship gatherings. Ephesians 5:19-20 declares, *"Speaking to one another in psalms and hymns and spiritual songs, singing and making melody with your heart to the Lord; always giving thanks for all things in the name of our Lord Jesus Christ to God, even the Father; and be subject to one another in the fear of Christ."* We need to be lifting up our voice and singing praise to Him at all times.

The word "doxology" also means to glorify. How are we suppose to glorify or praise God? No question is more significant. The supreme purpose in life for any man or woman - for anyone who has ever been born into this world— is to glorify God. That is what living for the Lord is all about.

Confession of sin glorifies God, because if you excuse your sin, you absolve yourself of responsibility and blame God for letting you get into a predicament. In Genesis, this is illustrated to us. Genesis 3:12 says, *"The man said, "The woman you put here with me--she gave me some fruit from the tree, and I ate it."* He was excusing his sin and blaming the Lord for it. To do that is to blame God and thus assign guilt to Him. God is never at fault, when we sin. Implying that God is somehow responsible—maligns His holiness.

1 John 1:9 says, *"If we confess our sins, he is faithful and just and will forgive us our sins and purify us from all unrighteousness."* The Greek word for "confess" is *homologeo,* meaning "to say the same thing." To confess means to agree with God that sin is all our fault and to repent. That act glorifies God. He is faithful and just to forgive as soon as we agree with Him.

Psalm 50:23 says, *"He who offers a sacrifice of thanksgiving honors me."* Praise honors God..

We may be unhappy with ourselves or unhappy in our circumstances. Who made us?... God. He promises to supply all our needs. When we are content, we acknowledge God's sovereignty in our lives and that gives Him glory. Philippians 4:11 says, *"I am not saying this because I am in need, for I have learned to be content whatever the circumstances."* Paul was confident that God would use all things- poverty as well as abundance, comfort as well as pain— for Paul's good and God's glory (Romans 8:28). In whatever circumstances we may be in, remember to always give the Lord the glory, because it will grow us in our walk with Him.

John 14:13 says, *"Whatever you ask in my name, that I will do, so that the Father may be glorified in the Son."* Praying in His name means praying in accordance with His character and His will. God delights to reveal His glory in answered prayer. He commands us to pray and to share our heart with Him. Let's praise God from whom all blessings flow!

To glorify God is to extol His attributes— His holiness, faithfulness, mercy, grace, love, majesty, sovereignty, power, and omniscience. Psalm 34:1 declares, *"I will extol the LORD at all times; his praise will always be on my lips."*

When we live to glorify God, He responds by giving us overwhelming joy! "Well," you say, "I have a tough life and I don't have any joy." May I suggest an answer? Start living for God. He is all that you need. He is your Portion and your Daily bread.

Joy does not necessarily always make sorrow, discouragement, pain, and failure go away, but because we have the Lord, we know that He is with us and will never leave us. To know that we have Him through the difficult times gives us peace and happiness.

Philippians 4:11 says, *"Rejoice in the Lord always. I will say it again: Rejoice!"* Let us rejoice in our Savior today!

God desires our whole heart. He longs for us to know the power of His presence over our lives. He desires to bless us more than we could imagine. His Spirit urges us onward, calling us closer. May the Lord help us to look up...open our mouths...and sing.

Our purpose in life is to glorify God in everything. 1 Corinthians 10:31 says, *"So whether you eat or drink or whatever you do, do it all for the glory of God."* May we sing and praise Him, so that He could be glorified and be honored. Everyday we get to praise the Lord. Our lives can be a "doxology"— a life that is pleasing to the Lord. A life that can praise Him to the utmost! Charles H. Spurgeon poignantly said, *"It is, perhaps, one of the hardest struggles of the Christian life to learn this sentence— "Not unto us, not unto us, but unto thy name be glory."* Our soul always needs to say, but unto Thy name always be the glory! Let's walk in the character of "Doxology" and have a passion to turn everything in our lives into worship, thus giving God glory in all things!

Doxology

Praise God, from Whom all blessings flow;
Praise Him, all creatures here below;
Praise Him above, ye heavenly host;
Praise Father, Son, and Holy Ghost.

Conclusion

Sing to him, sing praise to him;
tell of all his wonderful acts.
1 Chronicles 16:9

Let's seek to always praise and worship the Lord in every area of our lives. When we sing to Him, we will be blessed. Now is our time to sing to the Lord a new song. These hymns bring us closer to the Lord, when we come into His presence and sing praises to Him. I pray that we would not only sing these hymns, but the words would truly come from our heart. May we not only read these words, but my hope is that they would bring vibrant change into our hearts and our lives. So...let's sing!

God's heart for setting words to melodies is evident from the book of Psalms.

Psalm 96:1-2
"Sing to the Lord a new song;
sing to the Lord, all the earth. Sing to the Lord,
praise his name;
proclaim his salvation day after day."

Psalm 47:6

"Sing praises to God, sing praises; sing praises to our King, sing praises."

In just two Scriptures, we're commanded to sing seven times. The Bible contains over four hundred references to singing and fifty direct commands to sing. The longest book of the Bible, the Psalms, is a book of songs and praise. In the New Testament, we're commanded not once, but twice to sing psalms, hymns, and spiritual songs to one another when we meet.

Ephesians 5:19 says, *"Speaking to yourselves in psalms and hymns and spiritual songs, singing and making melody in your heart to the Lord."*

Colossians 3:16 states, *"Let the word of Christ dwell in you richly in all wisdom; teaching and admonishing one another in psalms and hymns and spiritual songs, singing with grace in your hearts to the Lord."*

We are a singing people, because it is how God has created us. The Lord is far less concerned with our melodic tune then our integrity. Worshipping the Lord begins with our heart, not on our lips. God wants us to sing and make music from our hearts to the Lord! We are created to sing, because it leads us joyfully to our magnificent Singer and Creator of the heavens and the earth. "God is the ultimate Musician. His music transforms our lives."[2] The lyrics of His grace and redemption transform our hearts. His songs of forgiveness, grace, truth, hope, sovereignty, and love bring us back to our original desire of praise to God.

When we are obeying God and His Word, we become compelled to sing. Worship comes from a deep desire in our hearts. It's about what and who we love more than everything else. Our desire to sing comes from the One who died and rose from the grave. "Worship is driven by a heartfelt desire to convey the Gospel Truth to those of us who already know it and need to be refreshed and renewed by it and to communicate it to those who don't yet know our King."[1] "We sing because we're created to, commanded to, and compelled to!"[1] When we sing truths, our hearts are changed and we come into His courts with praise on our lips."

Psalm 16:11
"In His presence, there is fullness of joy."

We must not only sing when we are happy. Singing hymns, worship songs, or psalms, can give us the greatest encouragement when we are in the midst of our darkest and hardest trials. They give us hope and renew our minds. We have the freedom to weep and to pour out our souls to a God who hears and answers our cries. Our singing can prepare and sustain us for each season of life that comes our way. Let us gaze on the truth that, because He lives we can face each day!

Martin Luther once said of music, *"Music is a gift and grace of God, not an invention of men. Thus it drives out the devil and makes people cheerful… The devil, the originator of sorrowful anxieties and restless troubles, flees before the sounds of music almost as much as before the Word of God."* "Singing helps us put on the Armor of God. It helps tighten the belt of truth firmly around our waist and the breastplate of righteousness on our chest; it readies our feet to bring the gospel of peace. It strengthens our muscles to hold the shield of faith and the sword of the Spirit in our hands, and steadies the helmet of Salvation upon our head."[1]

Remember today that the song in your heart will bring times of rest and joy to your soul. So, SING joyfully knowing that we are singing to the most holy and beautiful Musician of all. He is worthy of all our praise!

Psalm 35:28 declares
"And my tongue shall speak of your righteousness and of your praise all the day long."

Why does God, so often tell us not simply to praise Him, but to *sing* His praises when we meet? Why not just pray and preach? Why sing? Why are God's people throughout history always singing? Why words and music and not just words alone? Why does God want us to sing? The reason is that God himself sings. In Zephaniah 3:17 God exalts over his people "with loud singing." He wants us to worship and sing to Him and to lift up His name. He wants our lives to be filled with worship.

I recognize that God gives each of us different gifts and talents, but at the end of the day we are called, wanted, and expected to sing. God has commanded us to and if we want a blessed life, we need to obey the Lord. Even if you don't have an amazing voice, we are all a joyful noise to the Lord!

Psalm 100:1-2

"Make a joyful noise unto the Lord, all ye lands. Serve the Lord with gladness: come before his presence with singing."

Our lives should be a life of worship.. in every area we need to glorify Him.

On the eve of Jesus's crucifixion, Jesus sang hymns with His disciples. Matthew 26:30 says, *"And when they had sung a hymn, they went out into the mount of Olives."* Hebrews 2:12 says, *"Saying, I will declare thy name unto my brethren, in the midst of the church will I sing praise unto thee."* Ephesians 5 tells us that one of the effects of being "filled with the Spirit" is "addressing one another in psalms and hymns and spiritual songs, singing and making melody to the Lord with your heart" (verses 18-19). We serve a holy and loving Father who sings. So let us sing to the Lord and worship Him!

Let's seek the Lord earnestly in all these things and go deeper with Him in our understanding and experience of corporate worship each week. We need to pray for each other and to love one another. I pray that we would be filled with His spirit and that we would have a praise-filled life!

Let us pray these things:

1. That all our worship would be "from the heart"
2. That we would be radically God-focused and God-centered.
3. That the foundation of our lives would be God's Word.
4. That we would have a praised-filled life

Worship is desired and commanded by the Lord. For Believers in Jesus Christ, worship is the expected way of life. The perfect God, who has saved Believers from their sins is completely worthy of all worship, both in this life and for all eternity. Let us worship Him, for He is worthy of all honor and praise!

I am earnestly calling on the name of the Lord that you would see that He wants us to worship Him, praise Him, honor Him, and glorify Him. I hope that these hymns and stories made an impact on your life, as much as they have blessed my life and brought me closer to my Savior.

Johann Sebastian Bach said, *"The final aim and reason of all music is nothing other than the glorification of God and the refreshment of the spirit."* The reason for music and worship is nothing less than to glorify God!

May the focus and center of our lives be to sing to Him and glorify His name!

Psalm 95:1
"O come, let us sing for joy to the LORD, Let us shout joyfully to the rock of our salvation."

Remember... He always keeps us singing!

Appendix:
Scriptures On Worship & Singing

Psalm 104:33 *"I will sing to the LORD as long as I live; I will sing praise to my God while I have my being."*

Jeremiah 20:13 *"Sing to the LORD, praise the LORD! For He has delivered the soul of the needy one From the hand of evildoers."*

Psalm 145:3 *"Great is the LORD, and highly to be praised, And His greatness is unsearchable."*

Psalm 95:1 *"O come, let us sing for joy to the LORD, Let us shout joyfully to the rock of our salvation."*

Psalm 95:6 *"Come, let us worship and bow down, Let us kneel before the LORD our Maker."*

Psalm 99:9 *"Exalt the LORD our God And worship at His holy hill, For holy is the LORD our God."*

Psalm 100:1-5 *"Shout joyfully to the LORD, all the earth. Serve the LORD with gladness; Come before Him with joyful singing. Know that the LORD Himself is God; It is He who has made us, and not we ourselves; We are His people and the sheep of His pasture. Enter His gates with thanksgiving And His courts with praise Give thanks to Him, bless His name. For the LORD is good; His lovingkindness is everlasting And His faithfulness to all generations."*

Psalm 105:2 *"Sing to Him, sing praises to Him; Speak of all His wonders."*

2 Samuel 22:50 *"Therefore I will give thanks to You, O LORD, among the nations, And I will sing praises to Your name."*

Psalm 150:6 *"Let everything that has breath praise the Lord! Praise the Lord!"*

Colossians 3:16 *"Let the word of Christ dwell in you richly, teaching and admonishing one another in all wisdom, singing psalms and hymns and spiritual songs, with thankfulness in your hearts to God."*

John 4:24 *"God is spirit, and those who worship him must worship in spirit and truth."*

Ephesians 5:19 *"Addressing one another in psalms and hymns and spiritual songs, singing and making melody to the Lord with your heart."*

Psalm 146:1-2 *"Praise the Lord! Praise the Lord, O my soul! I will praise the Lord as long as I live; I will sing praises to my God while I have my being."*

Psalm 7:17 *"I will give to the Lord the thanks due to his righteousness, and I will sing praise to the name of the Lord, the Most High."*

Isaiah 25:1 *"Lord, you are my God; I will exalt you and praise your name, for in perfect faithfulness you have done wonderful things, things planned long ago."*

Psalm 86:9-10 *"All the nations you have made will come and worship before you, Lord; they will bring glory to your name. For you are great and do marvelous deeds; you alone are God."*

Hebrews 2:12 *"He says, "I will declare your name to my brothers and sisters; in the assembly I will sing your praises."*

Psalm 71:23 *"My lips will shout for joy when I sing praise to you— I whom you have delivered."*

Psalm 150:1-5 *"Praise the Lord. Praise God in his sanctuary; praise him in his mighty heavens. Praise him for his* acts of power; praise him for his surpassing greatness. Praise him with the sounding of the trumpet, praise him with the harp and lyre, praise him with timbrel and dancing, praise him with the strings and pipe, praise him with the clash of cymbals, praise him with resounding cymbals."

Psalm 135:3 "Praise the LORD, for the LORD is good; sing praise to his name, for that is pleasant."

Psalm 59:16 "But I will sing of your strength,   in the morning I will sing of your love; for you are my fortress,   my refuge in times of trouble."

Luke 4:8 "And Jesus answered him, "It is written, "You shall worship the Lord your God, and him only shall you serve."

Psalm 96:9 "Worship the Lord in the splendor of holiness; tremble before him, all the earth!"

Psalm 66:4 *"All the earth worships you and sings praises to you; they sing praises to your name."* Selah

Exodus 15:2 *"The Lord is my strength and my song, and he has become my salvation; this is my God, and I will praise him, my father's God, and I will exalt him."*

Psalm 71:8 *"My mouth is filled with your praise, and with your glory all the day."*

Psalm 138:5 *"And they will sing of the ways of the LORD, For great is the glory of the LORD."*

1 Chronicles 16:29 *"Ascribe to the Lord the glory due his name; bring an offering and come before him. Worship the Lord in the splendor of his holiness."*

Psalm 69:30 *"I will praise the name of God with a song: I will magnify him with thanksgiving."*

Notes:

1. Getty, Keith & Kristyn. Sing! How Worship Transforms Your Life, Family, and Church. Nashville: B& H Publishing Group, 2017. Print., p.10.
2. Ibid., p. 33.
3. Ibid., p. 83
4. Ibid., p. 22
5. Tripp, Paul. A Quest for More: Living for Something Bigger. Greensboro: New Growth Press, 2007. Print., p. 145.

Made in the USA
Middletown, DE
17 November 2019

78894387R00119